Beyond Reproach

Jenny Simpson

This book is dedicated to ALL those suffering domestic violence,
whether you are Male or Female.

ISBN 0 9548710 1 4 BEYOND REPROACH

British Library Cataloguing in Publication Data available

A novel demonstrating how **Psychological abuse** can be damaging for all those involved. All characters, places and/or organisations are purely fictitious. Any similarities to those living or dead are purely coincidental.

First published 2005
Published in the UK by Nil Desperandum (2004) Ltd.
www.reach-for-the-skies.co.uk

© Jenny Simpson 2005

Printed by The Danewood Press Ltd, Chelwood Gate, Sussex
01825 740302

References and other recommended reading material

Men Who Batter Women -1999 - Adam Edward Jukes a psychotherapist and group psychoanalyst in private practice, London.

Surviving Domestic Violence – 2000 - Elaine Weiss, ED. D – Voices of Women That Broke Free.

Getting Out – 2000 - Ann Goetting with Caroline Jory – Life stories of women who left abusive men

The Kid – 2004 - Kevin Lewis, A true story

The Charm Syndrome – 1998 - Sandra Horley

I know Why The Caged Bird Sings – 1969 - by Maya Angelou.

Why Me, Why This, Why Now -1994 – Robin Norwood.

Social Identity – 2003 - Richard Jenkins, Professor of Sociology at the University of Sheffield.

Compelled To Control – 2003 - Keith Miller

Personality and Dangerous- 2001 - David McCallum, Genealogies of Antisocial Personality Disorder.

Without Conscience - 1999 - Robert D. Hare, Phd.

Other books available:

Just Another Day, Lucy Day.   Nil Desperandum (2004) Ltd
Living with Spirit, Janet Stead.Nil Desperandum (2004) Ltd

Further contacts :

Rights of Women, 52-54 Featherstone Street. London EC1Y 8RT
Advice line 020 7251 6575/6(Tue–Thur 2-4pm and 7-9pm Fri 12-2pm)

National Domestic Violence Helpline: 08457 023468

Refuge in partnership with Women's Aid – Free 24 hour help line :
0800 2000 247
www.refuge.org.uk or www.womensaid.org.uk

NSPCC: 0800 800 500 (24 hr Child Protection hotline)
www.nspcc.org.uk

Childline: 0800 1111 (24 hr advice and support for young people)
www.childline.org.uk

Respect: 0845 122 8609 (Providing information & advice for people
who are abusive or violent).

The Advocacy Wheel and Deluth principle– www.ifcc.on.ca

Samaritans: 08457 90 90 90 (23 hr national helpline for people in
crisis)

Shelterline: 0808 800 4444 (24 hr advice on housing rights and
options)

NHS Direct : 0845 4647 (24 hr general medical advice)

<u>Introduction</u>

This book has been written in the trust it will help all those suffering from domestic violence.

When you enter a relationship it is based on intimacy, trust and honesty and should not become a devastating experience leaving deep scars for all concerned.

In its simplest form Domestic Violence is used by an abuser to gain complete control. Isolation follows and control becomes complete. Why? Because it is easier for them to blame someone else for their own inadequacies, rather than face the cause, and deal with the problem. This is called 'blame transference'.

By using a dual personality, abusers gradually switch from A-B. As charmer they gain trust and dependency; weakening their victims' resolve and often offer help and guidance in order to maintain an upper hand, then slowly intimidation follows. Comments about the way that you look, dress or think. They pretend they are able to tell what your thoughts really are, regardless of your view.
If this fails a new element emerges, one of violence, whether that be physical or mental, in which you are made to feel you provoked or deserved this in some way.

By isolating the victim from friends and family it becomes a twilight world where only those involved are aware of the truth. Misinformation is fed to outside parties by the victim, who fears reprisals and the abuser so eventually the twilight world becomes the norm. Fear is used to keep control for which there is no escape. By making fear the instrument of control it is easy to see why escape appears to be futile. All those around you are treated with great suspicion by the abuser and as victim, you are unaware of what story they may have been told.

If the abuser feels the control is weakening they intensify the control mechanisms in order to maintain dominance, which can be mental, physical or even financial.
In the case of psychological abuse, this is often followed by a threat or act of violence.

Denial by the abuser is common. Even if they admit brutality, they deny it is their fault, always finding excuses for their behaviour – work pressures, too much to drink, you.
Each time they feel they are losing ground they use emotional blackmail or abuse to bring back the controls.

Abusers also use jealousy to keep control, feigning that you should be flattered by their attempts to keep you away from other potential partners. Friends and family are treated as outsiders and must be fended off to enable the control to continue.

After a tirade of abuse one day, the abuser is able to rationalise this and become the charmer the next. Apologising for their behaviour one minute and then justifying it. Each tactic is used to make you feel completely insecure and submissive.
By transferring their own insecurities onto their partner, they regain control and you enter the honeymoon period. This can last for as long as three months but, as time goes on, the cycle gets shorter – an ever decreasing circle. Each time the abuser feels justified in carrying on with a new set of rules: staying out late, not bothering to phone, or staying away for days at a time, and so the cycle begins all over again.

By accusing you of lying the abuser feels it is within their right to apply the new set of rules to the relationship. You just become mesmerised, confused and forgetful, trying desperately to rationalise the abuser's behaviour in order to keep your sanity.
And the abuser will offer hope for change, to keep the cycle moving.
Finally you are accused of inflicting this upon yourself. It is always your fault and you are blamed at every opportunity for the abuser's emotional state.

Anyone living in the home becomes privy to the abuse and must eventually join to become the next victim.

For you, the weaknesses are exposed, making you vulnerable for.any future relationships and prone to repeat the patterns that you accept as normal. Furthermore the children who have witnessed such events become conditioned and are at risk of repeating the patterns themselves, making them prey for criminal elements, political activist groups and abusers...

If you don't break the patterns, you are the perpetual victim……..................................

Prologue

Somerset, England

I stood alone in a country lane in my stocking-feet. No money, no phone and a long way from home, I felt my brain had been squashed like a melon, with his words still ringing in my ears. If I'd been able to tell anyone I knew, they wouldn't believe me, yet there I was standing in the middle of nowhere. So what did I do to deserve this?

They say relationships are hard work but some are just plain impossible. Having opened my heart, it was now bleeding and throbbing in my chest as if about to explode.

What was weird was how he felt justified in continuing his onslaught. 'Just answer yes or no', he screamed and then surmised that, a no reply equals Yes, yes equals no, and no answer at all, equals yes or no, dependent on the question. And if that wasn't enough, he kept slamming on the brakes until I gave the answer he wanted, or thought was right, whatever right was, because I was long passed caring. Eventually my brain became mush and that's when I yelled 'let me out', which he did of course and then drove off.

Standing there in the middle of the lush green, Somerset countryside, a fitting poem popped into my head, by William Blake:

> **O Rose, thou art sick!**
> **The invisible worm,**
> **That flies in the night,**
> **In the howling storm,**
> **Has found out thy bed**
> **Of crimson joy,**
> **And his dark secret love**
> **Does thy life destroy.**

For many years, I was ashamed of my past and made to feel guilty. Having been encouraged to write about my experience by friends, I did so. And life couldn't have been better, my fiancé suggested we spoke about it, as he didn't want, what he described as secrets between us and this explains what happened, when I began to tell him of my life..

Chapter 1

Two years earlier, London

My life came full circle lately. Two failed long-term relationships, one physically abusive and the other – well, David just didn't believe me as far as my marriage to Andy was concerned, choosing to believe I'd provoked my husband in some way, which led to a downward spiral in our own relationship.

I had thought about my life's experiences and in particular, attributing fault. That was always going to be a tough one, we can all look back and wonder whether we could have handled things differently, and so guilt does form a part in that, and we do live in a blame society, so I found it better to say nothing, or even agree there are two sides to every story.

Anyway now David wants to meet, concerned I don't look for what he calls 'coincidences' during our years together.

> "You've got to get them young and keep them busy. Andy wasn't the smart one, it was you Jane".

"Really!", I said, looking confused, knowing full well I'd been too frightened to open my mouth in front of Andy, as it always progressed from a row to an escalation of violence. Grace still recalls the day he threw a television at me.

> "What do you mean get them young, and keep them busy?" I said.
> David laughed. "No, it's definitely you. I should never have taken you for a fool. You know revenge is a dish best served cold, don't you?"
> "Revenge on who and what for?" I said, looking even more

confused than usual.
He didn't answer, preferring to laugh again, shaking his head from side to side.

> "But I don't understand what you're talking about," I said,
> genuinely sounding frustrated and wondering if we spoke the
> same language. "Explain".

He ignored me, and started telling me about his recent holiday in Africa, where he'd met a woman, in her fifties, who having left London, started a business in Senegal, close to the borders of Gambia, growing hemp which she turned into cloth.
David had fallen in love with the place and was seriously considering moving there to start a business of his own, running a taxi service for the locals.

"I want to buy a Mercedes here and drive it over. There are lots of opportunities, Jane. I've already bought a plot of land for £4,000, and it's right next to the beach. It's really cheap out there. Then I'm going to put a small house on it."
"That's nice, I'm really pleased for you", I said still feeling confused and a little agitated by his earlier comment.
"Yep, I'm going to really make it, and then I'm going to buy me a Panama hat, I've always wanted one," he said, realising I wasn't paying attention.
"Look Jane, I haven't been able to cope with any thing too mentally in-depth. I can't analyse what went wrong with our relationship."
I shrugged my shoulders.
"It doesn't matter", I said. "We're just different people that's all."
He'd always lived a day-to-day existence believing the world owed him a living, as one of his friends once described him.
Borrowing money from friends and never repaying it.   In his mind everyone was there to be exploited.
He seemed to have forgotten it was my ailing company that had written a reference in order for him to get a full-time job…..................In fact he never thanked me for anything I'd done for him, strange. Anyway, that was all past now.
 He continued telling me about why he was leaving and his business idea and showed me photographs of his trip.

"This country's had it, everyone's going abroad to live. It's just too expensive here. If I had some assets to sell, I'd leave tomorrow. I only need £5,000, about the price of your car. You'd be pretty upset if it was stolen, wouldn't you Jane?" I smiled, I learnt to say nothing when David came out with these things. After all he knew I loved my red little sports car. But at least it's insured, I thought. David on the other hand was quite happy to drive around with dodgy paperwork and had no respect for the authorities. The odd thing was that without a mortgage or utility bills to pay, he was now pleading poverty.

He looked at me for a moment, his eyes narrowed and a frown appeared on his forehead.

> "Why don't you buy some shares in my new company? You could make a fortune, Jane."

> "No, thanks, I'm sure I couldn't afford it." I said firmly.

We both laughed nervously, trying to avoid each other's gaze, and it took several seconds before either of us spoke.

> "Did you ever love me, Jane?"

Wow, that was a difficult question to answer, especially now, so I lied.

> "Of course I did, still do in a way. Now I just want to see you happy..............You asked me to meet and told me not to look for coincidences. What did you mean by that?" I asked,

trying to bring the conversation back onto a subject that had awakened my curiosity. David took a deep breath,

> "I wanted to meet to see if you're OK. That's all. I heard your company had folded and you hadn't got any work right now. I was concerned for you. Forget what I said about coincidences, it was just an excuse to see you. Look, here's a photo of the beach and this is where Lucy, the lady I met lives. You'd like her and over here......."

My brain had already turned off, and I'd begun to concentrate on what was behind our meeting. As he continued I looked at him. What did I see in him? He had been reluctant to help me with anything over the past few years.

Pretending to act as a 'house-husband', during our relationship. However, he didn't much like housework and when I fell pregnant, as I was the only bread-winner, he was the first to suggest a termination, telling me he didn't really like kids. I already had one, Grace, who was ten when David and I first met.

One of acquaintances once confided in me, that she took a dislike to him after being told a story where he offered to fix an old lady's television and charged her £100 even though it was only a blown fuse in the plug. But what upset her the most, was that he found it amusing.

I had tried to encourage him but he didn't value my views due to my past and at times it was as if he didn't have a social conscience. Quite the contrary to the way I was brought up, which was to respect my elders.

There was little point in asking him to look in the mirror and face up to who he really was, cutting out the pretence, because honesty wasn't part of his remit, at least as far as I was concerned. He treated me like a small child with no understanding of life. Worst was he knew he wasn't right for me, I think he had known that from the beginning and although he ducked and dived the issues, turning them into a kind of game, it just wasn't one I was prepared to play any longer. Because that is exactly what it was and if anything I had found myself slipping into his world, where I knew I didn't belong.

I looked at him for a moment, his boyish looks were beginning to fade and there would come a day when he'd have to face reality.

I could feel my head nodding as I pretended to listen but I knew from his eyes, as they darted across my face that he was still trying to gain the upper hand and see what I was thinking.

"Our relationship would never be successful, Jane, too much has happened."

I continued nodding, forcing myself to wake as a glazed descended on my face. What on earth was I doing here? I guess I just expected too much, I thought he'd say sorry and we could talk about what went wrong and at least remain on amicable terms but just being here I was beginning to have serious doubts.

"I loved you very much but you just didn't believe me Jane." I nodded again, thinking really!!! I'm sure he cared in some way, I had become a habit, but loved!

I could see the lines on his face as he reached for another cigarette and realised I was making him nervous!

"Look", I said trying to think of something positive to say. "You could do something for me right now, write a letter to Grace and tell her it's not her fault."

He looked at me in complete astonishment. "What?!"

Andy, her father, had been quite vicious and the realisation David was just along for the ride was a difficult concept for her to accept. It has been bad enough for me to accept as an adult, but I wasn't about to give him the pleasure of seeing my pain. Equally, I was determined Grace shouldn't go through life thinking this was normal.

Children blame themselves when things go wrong. It certainly wasn't her fault. David was just an opportunist, and at the time I felt the world didn't want to know people like me and I've been beating myself up over it ever since. So if someone's to blame it's me.

David had never been interested in Grace, not really. He pretended they had a wonderful relationship, which I didn't understand. He was right about that and if I'm honest, I was probably too caught up in trying to earn a living to see how things really were. However Grace also covered things up, I knew she was angry at times and David would convince me she exaggerated the truth.

In reality Grace tried really hard to get him to like her, but was rebuffed and eventually gave up.

When Grace became a teenager she started to cheek him back, making him angry, and after all, as he would often point out, she wasn't his kid, so he felt he didn't need to try. He would accuse her of being lazy, criticising her at every opportunity and no matter how hard I tried to praise her it would be his comments and that of her father she listened to. As a result she started comfort eating and staying in her room.

It was as if my comments didn't count. I had become a non-person because of what she had seen her father do to me. As if she felt they were superior in some way and that she had to suffer, giving David the upper hand, which he wasn't slow to spot. He liked his own space and found her an irritant. When I questioned things he'd blame her entirely, and because she didn't trust me, it was difficult to know how to deal with the situation or even what the situation really was.

What a useful weapon he must have had; I was still trying to work things out, working long hours to give Grace a future with little or no support around me.

"But what on earth has it got to do with Grace?" David interjected, breaking my thoughts and making me jump back into consciousness.

"This is the longest relationship I've ever had! Look, Jane I know I've made some mistakes but I've never had a family before. I know I didn't contribute much financially but this relationship meant a lot to me."

Suddenly he was talking to me about his numerous past relationships and somehow I wasn't surprised.

"Jane, you've lasted longer than my marriage!!!"

But the burning question in my head was why had I wasted my life? I could feel myself losing my cool and knew this wasn't the time to start showing him I was upset. Men don't like emotional women, so I kept that thought firmly in my head.

"This isn't helping me much David. Where did you say your ex-wife lives?"

"Sussex. Hey, you'll like this one, she told me about two brothers who live there. They're really an amazing couple of wheeler-dealers. I bet they're worth a bob or two."

"Hmm" I took a deep breath. "What's so amazing about them?"
"Well, I could learn a lot from them, put it that way, now what about this letter?"

No wonder I was always confused. He hated it if anyone thought badly of him and was more concerned with what I might have told people, which seemed strange as I'd no intention of keeping in touch with any of his friends or family. I wanted a fresh start away from the past.
I took a notepad from my bag and tore off some sheets.

"Look do something good for a change. So much has happened in our relationship, just give Grace a chance to get her life together. Don't let her feel any guilt. She's been through enough already. It's no one's fault" I said.

"This is ridiculous, Jane, it really hasn't got anything to do with her"

I felt like saying look 'Bonzo' brain, you just spent several years as part of our family and although you didn't see it that way, maybe she did, but instead I said,

"It's easy, you left without saying goodbye. You were a part of her life for a number of years and you owe it to her. I wanted to give her a home where people respected and cared for one another; it didn't work out that way."

I felt like reminding him of the things Grace had told me. How he'd borrowed money from her when she came home from school, making out she didn't need it. How he'd punched her in the arm sometimes when she walked past him, because she'd been in his way. How he'd tried to shoot at her with an air rifle when she was in the garden because he didn't think, she was moving fast enough, and how he tried to set light to her with a cigarette lighter for amusement'.
Yes, he found it amusing and if you caught him doing something strange, he'd say it was a bit of a laugh, only now the laugh had come to an end. The tragic reality was Grace probably accepted this as normal because of her past experiences and that is something I have to live with.
I was just too caught up in things and didn't understand it myself, more importantly, I didn't have the time to sit and analyse.

Andy had continued to make things more difficult for me and it had taken five years to untangle myself from the business he and I ran during our marriage.

"Well, if it gets rid of the whole thing, let's do it." David said angrily.

I knew I was getting to him and he couldn't wait to write a letter exonerating himself. He took the pen and with my help put a letter together.

'Your life is your own to live. You'll make your own mistakes and errors along the way. Experience comes with age and we're all still learning as we go. The mistakes you make later on affect others around you; as much as you don't want that to happen, it does. All you can do is try to make the most out of every situation good or bad. Relationships are hard work, especially if they don't work out; you just got caught in the crossfire. Life has a habit of throwing up unforeseen obstacles along the way; all you can do is deal with them as best you see fit. Life as we know it doesn't last long, but you've got over the first hurdle relatively unscathed. All you need to know is, you are loved and respected and only the best things are wished for you. Once you know what it is you want to do, you'll get all the encouragement and backing you need.'

I thanked him. I knew he was going back to Africa at the end of the month and we were unlikely to meet again.

I don't think he realised, but I owed him a lot; not in any material way and certainly not in an emotional way. He just put a barrier between Andy and myself and the fog I'd been surrounded by for years was beginning to lift. Some might argue whether I really needed to know about life in this way. But its amazing how many friends and family you no longer have around you when you're going through a violent relationship, so without him the story wouldn't be complete.

When I got home, Grace, who was now sixteen, had taken herself off to her grandmother's, having first trashed my bedroom and leaving a note. She arrived back at 1.00 a.m., still furious.

"I don't understand why you went to see him!" she shouted angrily.

"Well, I can see you were upset by the state of my room," I said, trying to pick up the things scattered around the floor, then out of the corner of my eye, I spotted my laptop lying face down.

"Oh, no, not that!" My heart sank; that's all I need.

I picked it up and placed it on the dressing table and to my amazement it still worked.

"Why do you do it mum? you always attract men that use you. Why can't you choose a man who genuinely loves you? Do you enjoy being used?"

"No, Grace, it's just people", I retorted, trying to sound calm but at the same time feeling she's right, it's me! I am to blame.

Grace just looked, sneered and walked away.

I continued picking up the mess and watched as a crack emerged across the laptop screen. And as I sank into the nearest chair, a million thoughts rushed into my head. Suddenly I was back on my feet, charging after Grace, screaming at the top of my voice.

"You useless bitch, I'm going to make you pay for that. What am I going to do now? I use it for work. Are you going to go out and earn the money I need to pay the bills? No, of course not, you're happy making my life a misery. You can't even support yourself. You make me sick, you're just like your father. I wish I'd never married him and as for you..................." I stopped; Grace had turned white and had begun to shake. I closed my eyes as the words of her father echoed in my head 'you useless bitch you can't even bring up a child properly' and I walked back to my room where I sat down in front of the laptop and began reading the notes I'd started typing the night before.........................

What is our perception of 'normal'? In today's society with so many single parent families all we can hope for is that we give our children the knowledge to keep them on an even keel.

One of my favourite phrases has always been, "now let that be a lesson to you of what not to do."

I didn't set out to be a self sufficient, independent woman. I was driven by the need to survive, a primal animal instinct.

Grace popped her head round the door,

"I'm sorry mum. I didn't mean to break your laptop. I don't want to be like dad." Tears were rolling down her face.

"Let's not talk about it now, it's late and I've got work tomorrow and by the way you're not like your Dad. I just lost my temper that's all, but you really try my patience. We're all a bit raw right now. I've got this temp job starting tomorrow and I really needed the laptop."

"I'm sorry mum, can you fix it?" She said.

I laughed and took a deep breath. "Yeah sure, maybe, who knows, now just go to bed and we'll speak tomorrow" I said, biting my tongue.

That's how everyone viewed me, someone who fixed everything.

I was the bread- winner, paid the bills, cooked, washed, decorated. You name it I did it.

I lay on the bed, and my mind began to whirl around making me feel dizzy, I must have drifted off because when I awoke I could hear the rattle of the milk float and the milkman clattering the bottles on the doorstep. I heard Grace get ready. She was unusually quiet that morning but I was pleased we didn't speak, as it would give me time to think of what to say later.

I'd been taken on delivering IT training for accountancy software but felt, and looked like, I'd done a couple of rounds in the boxing ring. My head throbbed, my eyes were swollen and red and seemed to be bulging from their sockets. I dressed quickly and jumped into the car............ Pleeeease start. It spluttered and then roared as the engine kicked in. Brilliant, at least something works. I placed my battered laptop on the seat beside me and fumbled with the radio, searching for the nearest station. I could hear a Doris Day song intermittently playing as I tried to tune into the local news and traffic station ...."When I was just a little girl, I asked my mother what would I be. Would I be happy..........................."

> "Ah, there it is." I always liked to listen to the news, in case there
> was a traffic hold up somewhere.

I was already late, and, knowing my luck, there was bound to be a delay but to my surprise, it was a relatively easy journey. I'd worked all over the place, sometimes driving as much as two hours to work everyday and covering the length and breadth of the UK, so this job was a welcome relief, being only an hour's drive from home. I arrived at the building and quickly deposited my belongings and was greeted by a fellow colleague.

> "Jane, you're late. Come on, you've got a group of five today
> and the Chief Executive wants an hours private tuition at
> 12 O'clock sharp. He doesn't know anything about computers so
> start with the basics. You know, the on and off button, overview
> of the operating system, how to pick up e-mails and get onto the
> Internet, that sought of thing. He's using a laptop. I see you've
> brought one with you."
> "Yes, although it would be easier if he has one of his own that
> he's more familiar with," I said nervously waiting for the reply.
> "He does, it's on his desk and has already been set up for use."

I was ushered into a room where five staff eagerly waited.

> "Hello, my name's Jane. We're here to go through the new
> bespoke software system. I'll run through the basics and if you
> would like to take notes, then I can answer your questions later."

Time flew and it wasn't long before twelve O'clock had arrived and I was in the Chief Executive's office. He was described as an unapproachable man with quick temper. Although I found he had an inquiring mind and thirst for knowledge. He had a fourteen year old son and as soon as we'd dispensed with the basics, we went on-line, where I showed him how to explore the internet, using search engines. He was not only an attentive pupil, but a quick learner, making my job more enjoyable.

That evening Grace and I agreed it better to say nothing of the previous evening's events and I soldiered on with the laptop typing random notes and watching as the crack on the screen grew wider and started to turn black. I was finding it difficult to find the energy to hold things together and I don't mean the laptop.
Grace was becoming a very angry young woman. The problem was finding time to get her to understand her anger and trying to stop her directing it at me.
Conversations would end in 'slanging' matches with both of us retreating to our respective corners. The reality was, with the absence of her father and his complete denial of what happened, the only person she could have a go at was me.

Realising I was about to lose my laptop altogether, the following day I placed an order for a new screen. The price £300 + VAT, which excluded labour, so I decided to fit it myself.

From time to time one of David's friends would ring and give me an update. He did go back to Senegal, where they spoke French. He loved the language, having lived there some years earlier. By all accounts he was into the locally grown marijuana and enjoying himself, and had no intention of coming back .
His mum died when he was fourteen. Unfortunately no one though to tell him how ill she really was until she died, which was a terrible shock and kind of made him emotionally stuck. I guess that was why he would say, "if you haven't got anything, nothing can be taken away." The only problem with that is, it's ok if you only have yourself to think about but when you've got kids, you've also got responsibilities.
He'd often hinted about pulling off some deal or other and would ask me to get involved, but my answer was always no.

"You'll never get rich Jane", he'd say, as his contempt for me grew. "You've got some extra cash, why don't you sell up and buy a nice place in France. There's a guy I know out there, has a huge place with a fishing lake. He's building some chalets, which he rents out and charges people to fish, you could make a fortune! We could make a fortune"

The problem was our relationship was already on the rocks and the thought of moving further away from family and friends would just put Grace through more anguish.

My mind was drawn back to Grace, who throughout had just wanted to be accepted and understood.
We'd all let her down.
In some way she blamed herself for things that had happened but there was no blame. She was dealing with adults that didn't understand themselves.

I, on the other hand, no longer craved for a family life. I'd developed into an individual, with needs, wants and desires of my own, but it pained me that the warm family environment I had as a child wasn't achievable for Grace.

It wasn't long before I was unemployed again. That was the nature of being 'self-employed'. Contracts came and went.
However, the new screen for the laptop arrived, so I busied myself for the next four hours fitting it. And much to my surprise it worked!!
Grace was on half term and was impressed by my 'hidden' talent.

"You ought to start another business one day, Mum."
"Well, I keep trying but it just isn't working darling"
"But you're clever. You could do it, I know you could."
"At the moment, I need to work for other people to keep things ticking over and what I don't need is anymore breakages, understood?"
"I'm sorry I broke it, Mum. But I don't understand you sometimes."
"No probs, it's working now and when I saw David last he gave me a letter he had written for you. He just wanted to say goodbye. I'll give it to you later."

I had tried to set-up several small businesses but they weren't bringing in enough to pay the bills.

I'd previously set up a secretarial company, offering typing services to local companies but it failed when I ran out of time. I tried to keep going on all fronts, offering typing and CV's on Saturdays.

Before that I'd run my own company for 12 years, until things went wrong with Andy. Unfortunately that was difficult to come to terms with; who wants an ex-director of a company who can't even get a reference from her ex-husband. It's amazing how you find out who your friends are, when you haven't got any money.

I wouldn't have recognised it but my confidence had taken quite a bashing after my marriage and I'd made a complete mess of things with David. Still that's life, no one's perfect.

There was a knock at the door and an envelope fell through the letterbox. Inside was a note from David 'thought you might need this' It contained £150. 'Good luck, D'

Well it might pay the phone bill, I thought or maybe I should split it up and pay a bit off each of the credit cards. Oh, who knows. I comforted myself with the thought that at least the laptop was working and went to make a cup of tea by way of reward for my diligence. Whilst the kettle boiled I found myself staring out of the window. The garden was becoming a jungle and no matter how hard I tried, the brambles kept growing with a vengeance, entwining themselves around everything in their path. Must cut the grass at the weekend, if the weather's fine.

I pottered around doing the normal routine things, washing, cleaning, ironing and spending time with Grace and later that evening went to my room and toyed with the idea of writing a book, thus turning my random notes into something more tangible. Then I came across the drawings Grace had made when she was eight years old and realised she had been through so much and wondered how she had felt at the time.

Chapter 2

Friends had been trying to get me to turn my notes into a book for years, then someone suggested I try writing my life in five paragraphs, equivalent to five chapters.

So here goes,

      1.Born 1956. Went to primary school, went onto the local comprehensive, left school at sixteen.

      2.Got a job in a local garage for 6 months then joined a computer software company.

      3.Marrried Andy, an Electronics engineer.

      4.Grace was born

      5.Andy wanted me to be at home with Grace, so gave up work. But now he treats me like a slave.

      6.Andy criticises everything I do.

      7.Andy starts to lose the plot and starts drinking. He's always been jealous and possessive and doesn't like me going out.

      8.Andy treats me like dirt and starts hitting me in front of Grace

joins   9.I start a business. Andy then gets sacked from his job and the company and now I am treated like a slave again

      10. Violence escalates, so get divorced, which takes seven years to implement because Andy refuses to co-operate with anything.

      11. Meet David, after going to meet a girlfriend who tells me she is in distress. He gets to know me realises I have a problem with my ex and eventually moves in to protect me from Andy's outbursts.

      12. No violence this time but I am still expected to do everything or maybe I'm just used to it?

I looked at the clock, it's 1.00 am and I've written twelve items. The idea was to pull all the notes into each of the categories. I left the laptop and lay on the bed fully clothed, pondering about the mess my life was in and the unfathomable notes I'd just made and the mammoth task of turning any of it into something legible. I started writing in 1988, so piecing all those pieces of paperwork together was a daunting task and I had no idea how I was going to make any sense of it?

The sun shone through my bedroom window. I don't remember falling asleep but must have slept soundly because my head was all groggy.

I showered, dressed as usual and began to sift through the mountain of paperwork I'd been avoiding, namely the bills.
Half term was soon over and Grace was now back at school.

Oh, my God is that the time! Grace was a nightmare to get out of bed.
"You've got half an hour before we leave if you want a lift, if not you'll have to walk," I yelled. And watched as she pulled the pillow further over her head.

I then had a flash of inspiration, grabbed a copy of the local telephone directory and looked up language schools. I rang the number and asked whether they needed board for students.
"We'll put you on our waiting list. We need to take some further details then send someone round to inspect the type of accommodation you have to offer. You will need to provide the student with breakfast and an evening meal and treat them like a member of the family. If you're approved, we pay £90 a week per student."
"In that case, I'll take two" I said gleefully.
"Let's slow down a bit, first we need your name and address."
I hurriedly gave the details, and as I put the phone down, I turned round to find Grace staring at me. I realised she thought I'd lost my marbles.
"No more weird people, please Mum."
"It's OK, trust me."
I knew my words would fall on 'deaf ears', after all how could she trust me.
My reasoning was quite simple, I didn't want Grace to have a jaundiced view of people and in particular men and I also needed the money. So by bringing more people into our lives and making money in the process, I was confronting both issues at once.
Although I had to admit it was going to be difficult having complete strangers in the house.
"Let's go," I shouted as Grace sauntered out to the car. She could be extremely negative and stubborn at times. She never quite understood I was working for her benefit and just needed her to trust again.

After a few weeks our first student arrived, a young Italian called Lorenzo. A tall, good-looking young man, who captured Grace's imagination and for the first time ever, I saw a sparkle in her eye. He stayed with us for three weeks and brought a real sense of joy into the house. At the end of which Grace and he exchanged email addresses and have been corresponding ever since.

Following Lorenzo, came another Italian, Mr Gialli. Unfortunately he was a completely different 'kettle of fish'. He was what you would call a 'mature student'. At the ripe old age of forty-seven, he had come to London to study English and was a translator by trade.

His first observations were about the cooking, which was never quite to his liking.

"I would like to point out that you've put bread on the table. You never serve bread with pasta!" he exclaimed. "It's incredible to see such lack of organisation. I've heard the English were no good at cooking but this is preposterous."

I was a little shocked by his comments, having served a pasta dish with fish, fresh herbs and a light dressing accompanied by olive bread.

I had a keen interest in Mediterranean cooking and was open to criticism but not in the way this was delivered. However, I bit my tongue and politely replied

"Don't worry, you don't have to eat it, Mr Gialli. I would hate to force you to eat something you disliked."

He looked a little put out by my comment, but composed himself, lifting his head to stare momentarily at the ceiling, whilst contemplating what next to say.

"As I am to become part of your family for the next few weeks, please tell me something about yourself. For example, what music do you like?"

"Of course. Well, I like Rock mainly and funky Jazz but I have quite a lot of different types of music that I play dependent on my moods. For example I love Mozart, Classical is so soothing."

"Jazz!" He snapped back "Don't you know anything! Jazz is a disorganised mess." he raised his hands into the air, which made him look almost comical. "I prefer chamber music myself and I listen to nothing else, so maybe you could tell me where I can listen to this type of music in this country. Tomorrow will do. Now I must discuss with you the arrangements for my stay. I would expect you to do my washing and ironing. My sister does all of this for me in Italy, I haven't the faintest idea how to use a washing machine."

I looked at Grace, followed by the ceiling, then the floor, trying desperately not to laugh.

"I see", I said "well, this is going to be quite an education for you. We'll teach you."

His face turned to thunder and we ate the remainder of the meal in silence.

Grace helped remove the plates from the table and whilst in the kitchen, we agreed; Mr. Gialli had to go.

We returned to the dining room, where Mr Gialli announced:

"This is going to work out splendidly. I like to rise early around 7.30 am and bathe. I take it there's a TV in my room?"

"Yes there is." I said still trying not to laugh.

"Hmmm, I should like to retire now, would you please show me to my room."

Mr Gialli seemed elevated with the idea that he'd controlled the conversation, making reassuring remarks to himself in Italian and rubbing his hands together, whilst he followed me to his room.

I returned to find Grace shaking her head.

"You're not going to let him stay are you? Please, don't Mummy. I don't like him."

She was right, the thought of sharing our home with Mr Gialli for three weeks was unthinkable.

"Don't worry Grace, I'll get him to leave. Now get off to bed. I'll deal with it in the morning."

"I'm not going to be able to sleep with that creep in the house"

"Just bolt your door Grace, I'll have a word first thing in the morning with the college."

"Excuse me, I 'ave a problem, can you come 'ere" Mr Gialli was standing at the top of the stairs and even his voice was beginning to make me squirm.

"I cannot reach the light, it's too difficult for me and I can't see the switch, can you help me?"

To accommodate Mr Gialli's wishes, I followed him to his room and lent across the bed to turn off the light. And then realised how foolish I had been, after all, the switch was luminous green and could easily be seen in the dark.

"Goodnight, Mr Gialli."

"Goodnight", he said with a smile on his face.

The following morning I rose early to greet him.

"Good morning, Mr Gialli. I have already laid the table, there is cereal and toast and I've made some coffee. In future, I will put these out the night before, and all you have to do is heat up the coffee. Now if you would like to follow me to the kitchen, I'll show you where everything is and how it works. This is the washing machine. It's really quite simple. Here we go, you open the door like this and place your dirty washing inside, then close the door. You pull out this compartment and, by using the dispenser provided, measure out the right amount of soap powder. You then press the start button, couldn't be easier. Did you get that? If not, don't worry, I'll write it down."

"But this is outrageous! I pay you a weekly amount" he remonstrated.

"Correction, you don't pay me anything. The college pays a weekly amount, and in return I treat you as part of my family. I've checked the terms under which you're staying with us. I prepare you an evening meal and a packed lunch, as required. You will do all your own washing and ironing and I provide you with the tools to do so. The iron is over there, next to the ironing board.

Is that clear?" I turned and stared hard at Mr Gialli, whose face had turned red as he hurriedly walked away to the dining room, where he ate his breakfast in complete silence. He then gathered his belongings and left for college, scowling at me as he went.

I knew the college would call and around midday they rang to say that Mr Gialli was unhappy with his present accommodation. They listened attentively as I explained what had happened and to my amusement told me not to worry they'd already had a full dose of Mr.Gialli and were finding it difficult to get him to understand that if he wanted extra services he should pay for a hotel. It was agreed that Mr Gialli remained with us until they could find him somewhere else to stay, which became quite difficult as we all tried to avoid each other. But after a couple of days, a new home was found and a taxi sent to collect Mr. Gialli.

"Your taxi's, outside." I said, having answered a knock at the door.

"Then would you take my luggage please? I have a lot of things to collect and I don't want to forget anything"

"I'm sorry, I can't do that, Mr Gialli."

Mr Gialli took a deep breath as if I was trying his patience.

"Then kindly tell the taxi driver to collect them" he snapped.

Unfortunately, the taxi driver overheard Mr Gialli's comments, having returned to enquire why it was taking so long. He smiled, shook his head, rolled his eyes and whispered he would wait in the cab. I nodded in agreement.

"I'm afraid he can't do that Mr Gialli, he's waiting in the cab."

Eventually Mr. Gialli emerged, luggage in tow and the last image I have was of him staggering down the drive under the weight of suitcases, indignant that he, of all people should be treated in this way.

However, he was replaced by a young Belgian student, called Lionel, who was not only happy to join in as one of the family but even mowed the lawn for me. Grace was pleased I'd made a stand with Mr. Gialli and invited Lionel to accompany her and friends to the cinema, so peace had again resumed in our household.

Time certainly flies. It's the year 2001 and David is now a distant memory. Grace still sees Andy from time to time, and that's still a problem, as she rarely wants to spend much time in his company.

He's been in a relationship for sometime but still drinks quite heavily and has no regard for the drink driving rules. His girlfriend seemingly doesn't want to know Grace when she goes over to their flat, instead she shuts herself in her room, whilst Andy leaves Grace to play on his computer and watches sport on TV. I often get a call or text from Grace asking me to collect her, because she is bored or frightened of getting into the car with him.

Unfortunately, due to the nature of the beast, it is exactly at these times that Andy would insist on driving just to prove a point, without due regard for Grace, his own life or other people's.

Needless to say the visits are becoming few and far between. Andy blames me for this, always failing to see his own part to play.

It didn't take long before I began to feel the benefit from the extra income and was able to clear most of my debts. Ad hoc work was coming in and I've been offered another part-time job as a business advisor to small companies in the area.

Grace left school much to my annoyance but started work three days a week as a cleaner. She pays rent for her room and so with the extra money I pay for her to have driving lessons.

House prices have risen and I'd be foolish not to consider the possibility of moving out of London, thus ridding myself of the mortgage.
I no longer feel safe living here, there's just too much anger and too many memories.

Street crime and road rage is on the increase and I've experienced a few situations, which have been quite unnerving, and I worry for Grace.

One evening, whilst sitting at a set of traffic lights deep in thought, I was aware of a man walking across the road to the central reservation, but instead of passing behind the car, he grabbed the door handle and tried to get into the backseat. Luckily, my elbow was resting near the central locking button and when I heard the noise of the door being opened I pressed it, locking all the doors. I always had a habit of leaving my car in first gear and although the lights were red, I instinctively pressed the accelerator sounding my horn as I went, not waiting to see what happened.

There seemed little point ringing the police. I'd lost faith in the legal system sometime ago during my marriage to Andy. You were on your own but I can't help thinking how lucky I was.

Two weeks later I read in the local newspaper that another woman hadn't been quite so lucky. A man did get into the back seat of her car, carrying a briefcase. She was so terrified she drove into a tree, both fled the scene and later the police recovered a briefcase containing some rope and a knife.
Maybe David is right, time to move but where?
My sister wanted me to move nearer to her, but Grace has never been that keen. She lives in the countryside and Grace was worried about being cut off from her friends.

Grace is becoming a bit of an introvert lately, especially after her visits with Andy. He has tried to convince her the violence she saw as a child didn't take place. He never could face the truth and denial is his way of dealing with it. Unfortunately, for Grace those images were real and she's finding it difficult to come to terms with them, especially as Andy is still verbally abusive and sets off those emotional buttons in Grace sending her back to a past she would rather forget.

I was interrupted in my thoughts by the telephone. The caller took a deep breath and then put the receiver down. Over the past year I've received a series of weird calls to add to my worries.
Companies phoning from Africa, wanting me to ship out goods and strange men who are rude and then put the phone down. One caller told me I didn't know what it was like to suffer, as people in Africa have done. The world's certainly a mess nowadays but it's not just Africa suffering is everywhere.

I called my telephone provider.

"We get a lot of these complaints madam, but there are things we can do nowadays. We have a nuisance call line, for this kind of thing, I'll put you through."

Well, at least I am not alone.

I now have a number to put into the phone when I receive a call, which sends a message to the caller telling them I've barred their number. The wonders of technology!

Chapter 3

The notes on the laptop have become more random than usual, as if I might learn something about myself or even the age long question - the meaning of life?! In doing so, I have collated some famous quotes and poetry, which I've found amusing, melancholy, uplifting and enlightening.

"Desiderata"
Go placidly amid the noise and haste, and remember what peace there may be in silence. As far as possible, without surrender be on good terms with all.
Speak your truth quietly and clearly; and listen to others, even the dull and ignorant; they too have their story.

Avoid loud aggressive persons, they are vexations to the Spirit. If you compare yourself with others you may become vain and bitter, for always there will be greater and lesser persons than yourself. Enjoy your achievements as well as your plans.

Keep interested in your own career, however humble; it's a real possession in the changing fortunes of time.
Exercise caution in your business affairs, for the world is full of trickery. But let this not blind you to what virtue there is; many persons strive for high ideals; and everywhere life is full of heroism.

Be yourself. Especially do not feign affection. Neither be cynical about love, for in the face of all aridity and disenchantment it's perennial as the grass.

Take kindly the counsel of the years, gracefully surrendering the things of youth. Nurture strength of spirit to shield you in sudden misfortune. But do not distress yourself with imaginings. Many fears are born of fatigue and loneliness.
Beyond a wholesome discipline, be gentle with yourself.

You are a child of the universe, no less than the trees and the stars; you have a right to be here. And whether or not it's clear to you, no doubt the universe is unfolding as it should.
Therefore be at peace with God whatever you conceive him to be, and

whatever your labours and aspirations, in the noisy confusion of life keep peace with your soul.
With all its sham, drudgery and broken dreams, it's still a beautiful world. Be careful. Strive to be happy.

Max Ehrmann Found in old St.Paul's church Baltimore.
Dated 1692

The Invitation

It doesn't interest me what you do for a living,
I want to know what you ache for
And if you dare to dream of meeting your heart's longings.
It doesn't interest me how old you are
I want to know if you will risk looking like a fool for love,
For your dreams, for the adventure of being alive.
It doesn't interest me what planets are squaring your moon,
I want to know if you have touched the center of your own sorrow,
If you have been opened by life's betrayals or
Have become shriveled and closed from fear of future pain.
I want to know if you can sit with pain - mine or your own
Without moving to hide it, or fade it or fix it.
I want to know if you can be with joy - mine or your own
If you can dance with wildness and
Let the ecstasy fill you to the tips of your fingers and toes
Without cautioning us to be careful, be realistic
Or remember the limitations of being human.
It doesn't interest me if the story you are telling me is true.
I want to know if you can disappoint another to be true to yourself,
If you can bear the accusation of betrayal and not betray your own
soul.
I want to know if you can be faithful and therefore trustworthy.
I want to know if you can see beauty even when it's not pretty every
day
And if you can source life from God's presence.
I want to know if you can live with failure - yours or mine
And stand still on the edge of the lake and shout to the silver of the
moon, "yes!"
It doesn't interest me to know where you live or how much money you
have,
I want to know if you can get up after a night of grief and despair,
Weary and bruised to the bone to do what needs to be done for the
children.
It doesn't interest me who you are or how you came here.
I want to know if you will stand in the center of the fire with me and not
shrink back.
It doesn't interest me where or what or with whom you have studied.
I want to know what sustains you from the inside when all else falls
away.

I want to know if you can be alone with yourself and if you truly like the company you keep in
The empty moments.
By an Indian Elder

Earth has not anything to show more fair:
Dull would he be of soul who could pass by
A sight so touching in its majesty:
This city now doth, like a garment, wear
The beauty of the morning; silent, bare,
ships, towers, domes theatres and temples lie.
Open unto the fields, and to the sky;
All bright and glistening in the smokeless air.

Never did sun more beautifully steep
In his first splendour, valley, rock or hill;
Ne'er saw I, never felt, a calm so deep!
The river glideth at his own sweet will:
Dear God! The very houses seem asleep;
And all mighty heart is lying still!

**William Wordsworth, composed upon Westminster Bridge 3rd
September 1802**

We cannot live, except thus mutually
We alternate aware or unaware,
The reflex act of life:and when we bear
Our virtue outward most impulsively,
Most full of invocation, and to be
Most instantly compellant, certes there
We live most life, whoever breathes most air
And counts his dying years by sun and sea:
But when a soul, by choice and conscience, doth
Throw out her full force on another soul,
The conscience and the concentration both
Make mere life, Love. For life in perfect whole
And aim consummated, is Love in sooth,
As nature's magnet-heat rounds pole with pole.

E.B.Browning

The 1000th Man

One man in a thousand Solomon says,
Will stick more close than a brother.
And it's worth while seeking him half your days
If you find him before the other.
Nine hundred and ninety-nine depend
On what the world sees in you,
But the Thousandth Man will stand your friend
With the whole round world agin you.

Tis neither promise nor prayer nor show
Will settle the finding for"ee
Nine hundred and ninety-nine of em go
By your look or your acts or your glory.
But if he finds you and you find him,
The rest of the world don't matter;
For the Thousandth Man will sink or swim
With you – in any water.

You can use his purse with no more talk
Than he uses yours for his spendings,
And laugh and meet in your daily walk
As though there had been no lendings.
Nine hundred and ninety-nine of em call
For silver and gold in their dealings;
But the Thousandth Man he's worth em all,
Because you can show him your feelings.

His wrong's your wrong, and his right's your right,
In season or out of season.
Stand up and back it – in all men's sight
With that for your only reason!
Nine hundred and ninety-nine can't bide
The shame or mocking or laughter,
But the Thousandth Man will stand by your side
To the gallows-foot..........and after!

Rudyard Kipling

Chapter 4

Luckily for me the phone rang before I became completely immersed..

"Hi, Jane, what are you up to?" It was Adrian, the town centre manager. I remember how he'd turned up at my doorstep one day out of the blue, and asked if I would like to join a local business forum and through his contacts I also volunteered to join a local steering group. So now when I wasn't busy trying to earn a living, I did some voluntary work in the area and sat on a Steering Group, which basically met once every three months to discuss the proposed development of a multiplex cinema on a site I've known since a child. However, there was strong local opposition. Although my philosophy was that after years of nothing to replace the once magnificent building, anything that could bring this ruin back to life would clearly benefit the area as a whole. There had been several attempts over the years, but each one had fallen by the wayside. I have to admit the design was, in most people's eyes far too modern but so was its predecessor, maybe a cinema doesn't come close to the glorious history of the place but we live in modern times and were assured by the developers that the internal structure could be altered to suit a variety of uses.

The original building, a Victorian masterpiece, housed the arts, inventions, and textiles, to name but a few. **It's inventor disliked war, and believed that as science and invention crossed frontiers, to help them was also to help peace.**

Mathematicians on the other hand calculated the building would blow down in the first strong gale: engineers said the galleries would crash in and destroy visitors. Doctors thought that because there would be so many people coming to view its contents, there would be another outbreak of the "Black Death." Nevertheless the project was finished and was a great success...

I realised my mind had covered a multitude of things and that Adrian was awaiting my reply:

"I keep myself busy Adrian, and you?"

"Yes me too. Look, I've got a company who could really do with a hand. They can't pay you anything but they desperately need some advice on marketing."

"You mean you want a favour?"

"Well, yes I do Jane, it would only take a few hours of your time. You still get paid for the other work, don't you?"

"Ok, yes, I get the idea, give me their details and I'll see what I can do."

I alternated between working with a local business group, run by the council, running my own small business and voluntary work. I was happy to help Adrian out once in a while, in fact I quite enjoyed it, it was my way of giving something back. I liked meeting people, having run a secretarial service working with small business, it was an enjoyable challenge.

This wasn't the first time I'd been asked to do a favour; a few months ago he asked me to visit a local pet shop. The couple had invested all their savings from a life insurance policy they received after their son had been murdered. Unfortunately, they'd been struggling ever since. They hadn't looked at the market trend and as a result had bought the wrong stock. In the three hours I spent with them, they took a grand total of £3.99. As they had already been going some eighteen months, there was little I could do to change their immediate cash problems. However, not to be deterred, I went away and designed a leaflet, running off some 500 copies free of charge, and incorporating some of the ideas we had discussed.

"Don't worry Jane, it's not like the pet shop."

"You obviously read my mind, OK what's the name of the company?"

"It's Lansdown Ltd, they are just down the road from you. They've already been given financial advice from another advisor, you might know him, Richard Hooper?"

"Yes, I do, he's a very nice chap and I'm sure he's given them some sound advice, so why do you want me to talk with them?"

"Well, if you could just give us an overall view of the situation, Jane, it might help."

"Sure, just a minute and I'll grab a pen." I took down the details and promised to arrange a meeting.

But first things first, having decided that moving might be a good idea, I placed the house on the market.

I then rang Lansdown, who ironically had also been established some 18 months earlier and arranged to meet with the directors, Robert Wilson and Nick Jones. Robert told me they had a backer who'd invested in the company and provided them with offices at a cheap rent. The backer, Rupert Harding owned 30% of the company and was a local builder. He also had a backer, a South African businessman, and represented his interests in the UK. They already had a legal advisor, so it was only a matter of helping to market their ideas.

Robert came to the door.

"Hi, Jane, come through, I'd like to run something past you. It's a deal we're trying to put together offering decommissioning services for redundant computer equipment to a large insurance company. We need your help, I understand you were in IT components, is that right?"

"Yes, although it was a long time ago." We went through the concept and as I had some spare time I offered to type up the agreement, dictated by their legal advisor, Matthew.

"I've had to give the bank a personal guarantee, you know," Robert told me quietly. "But I'm not worried because I don't have any assets," he chuckled and then looked seriously at me again. "We just need to pull off one good deal. I'm confident about the insurance company, I've got a friend there and he thinks he can swing it in our favour."

"That's good, it's always helpful if you can build a rapport with your client." I said trying to sound authorititive.

I spent the remainder of the day typing and listening to their ideas, during the course of which, we spoke about the area in which we lived and how it was such a shame that so much of our past was being destroyed to make way for blocks of flats.

"I have always had a keen interest in Victorian property and the history associated with it.." I said

"Then you really ought to meet a friend of mine Alan Sedgewick", said Robert "I'm sure you two would get on, he also has a love for old property."

"Really? You know, so many of these properties are being demolished and eventually we won't have any to remind us of the past. There's a property just up the road from me, and it's been empty for about eight years now. There's even a tree growing through the middle, can you imagine that? It's rumoured locally, that the Housing Association neglected it, so they could demolish it at a later date. I like to think that's not true but it does make you wonder."

"Look speak to Alan. I'm sure he would try and help if he could. He's very well connected. Why don't I arrange for you to meet when he's next in the area?"

"That would be lovely, Robert, although I'm doubtful due to the time that has already elapsed but I would be happy to speak with him."

I finished typing and bade them farewell.

A couple of weeks passed before I received a call from Robert.

"Hello Jane, how are you?"

"I'm fine thanks, what can I do for you?"

"Well, I told you I would give you a call when Alan was next in the area and he's coming up to see me this morning, would it be convenient to pop in and maybe take a look at the property?"

"Umm.............let me just check my diary. One moment Robert........Yes, that's OK. What time?"

"Well, I can come round about 11.00 and Alan is making his way over from another appointment, so he'll probably arrive, around 11.30- 12.00. Is that OK?"

"Yes, fine, I'll have the coffee on, see you in a couple of hours."

"Look forward to it Jane."

Robert arrived first and had been at the house for nearly half an hour before Alan arrived. Alan was a man in his mid to late fifties. He had dark hair and brown eyes and seemed genuinely pleased to meet me. And strangely enough, I felt we had already met because his gushing approach took me quite by surprise. He came over, and shook my hand warmly.

"Pleased to meet you, I'm Alan Sedgewick Robert has told me so much about you."

"He has?" I said quizzically. "Would you like to come through, Robert is already here. Can I get you a coffee?"

"Yes, thank you, milk, and one sugar."

It was clear both men knew each other quite well and I left them talking about motor bikes, whilst I went to the kitchen to make the coffee.

Alan was the first to speak when I returned.

"Robert tells me you have a property that may be of interest? I pay an introductory fee of 3% on any successful purchase."

"Fine, it's just up the road. We can wander along after we've finished our coffee." I placed the cup on the table next to Alan.

"You've got a nice place here and I understand from Robert, you're also trying to sell"

"Actually, I already have a possible buyer." I said.

"I see, well if you get any difficulties or I can help in any way, I expect Robert has already told you, I'm in the property market."

"Thanks, I'll keep that in mind." I said being a little dismissive as that wasn't the reason he was here.

Robert was more interested in motor sports, and entertained us with stories of his younger days behind the wheel of a racing car. With coffee out of the way, I picked up the door keys.

"Shall we go?"

"Out of interest Jane, how much is a property like this worth?" Alan asked.

"It's been valued but I wasn't happy with the price, so I've advertised it on the Internet and have had some interest." He looked puzzled.

"If you like I'll come round some estate agents with you. It's always useful to get a feel of prices in the area." he said.

"If you like", I said nodding in agreement, as I continued walking toward the front door.

The property in question, was a short walk from the house and was in a terrible state. Eight years of neglect had certainly taken their toll.

"Can you find out who owns the property?" Asked Alan.

"I already have, it's owned by a Housing Association. Didn't Robert tell you that?"

Robert shook his head and smiled, "Sorry, I forgot."

"Do you know if it's been ear-marked for demolition?" Alan enquired.

"I'm afraid I don't but I wouldn't be at all surprised" I replied.

"Well it would be worth checking. Can you ring the local council and find out some more information?"

"Yes, I can certainly do that for you."

"Good, that's agreed then. Here's my telephone number and e-mail, give me a call when you have some more news. And remember, if there is any other land or property available, I would be interested and don't forget the introduction fee."

"Sure", I said as I started walking back to the house.

I could sense Alan looking at me intently as we made our way back, whereupon he got into his car, a white Volvo, strangely with moss growing on the roof. I could see a white Panama hat resting in the rear window, which amused me as I remembered how David had always said he'd like to get one.

"Thanks for coming, and I'll be in touch as soon as I have any news"

"OK, excuse the car, I just don't trust London, so I drive this beaten up old thing. It's pretty rough up here."

He drove off and I turned and said goodbye to Robert, agreeing to pop by the office during the week.

I then ran a bath, feeling the need to pamper myself for a while, and submerged myself beneath the bubbles, soaking up the warmth and staring at the ceiling, thinking, Life is really strange.

I wondered if Alan Sedgewick was indeed the genuine article, having heard about property developers. I laughed to myself and dismissed the idea because I needed to look at it purely as a way of earning some extra income.

Where did the day go? It was already three O'clock and I still had lots to do before Grace got home.

The following day I managed to complete my tasks and rang Robert to see if he would like me to pass by as I was just round the corner from his office. He was setting up yet another service, this time offering IT training and had wanted to know if I was interested in running a course on basic computer literacy. Never one to turn work down, I said I'd be happy to participate and assist them in getting the information together to produce a leaflet. I also put them in touch with a possible sales rep, who having contacted me over another matter, had impressed me by his spontaneity and wit.

"We would really like you to be more involved here, Jane we'll even pay you a salary."

"I appreciate the offer, Robert but I don't think you have the finances right now. So I'll pop in and lend a hand from time to time but I do have to continue with my other work but thanks for the thought. Anyway you know I'm likely to be moving away from the area."

"I'll miss you, where will you go Jane?"

"I haven't thought that far ahead yet but I do have people pulling me in different directions. My sister wants me to move nearer to her"

"Well, all I can say is the offer's there if you want it."

"Ok, thanks Robert, I'll keep it in mind."

I left the office feeling uneasy. Things didn't add up. Robert was always talking about the lack of finances and now he's just offered me a job. Last time we met, he hinted he wanted me to become more involved by way of shares in return for investment.

Back at base, I made a few notes and concentrated on some of the other companies I had been dealing with. I had three on my books at the time, each with their own set of unique problems.

A couple of days later, I got a call from Alan.

"Hello Jane, how are you? It's been some time. Did you have any luck with the Housing Association?"

"Yes I did, I was going to give you a call. It seems the property is due for demolition, and there's nothing anyone can do. I'm afraid the property has gone too far to be saved. Sorry about that, complete waste of time in the end."

"That's a shame. Have you got anything else for me to look at?"

"Well, that all depends on how big you want to go, there's a 12 acre site available. And if you give me a minute there's also a factory available for redevelopment"

I gave him the address of the factory, which had been up for sale for quite some time.

"Thanks Jane, I'm also interested in the 12 acre site. I wouldn't mind having a look at that. Can we meet?"

"Well, I can certainly show it to you when you are next in the area"

"How are you placed for next Wednesday Jane?"

"Next Wednesday sounds good, say 2.00 pm?" I made a note in my diary.

"That's fine, I look forward to seeing you."

Wednesday came round all too quickly and Alan arrived on his motorbike.

"Have you ever been on one of these?"

"No, I can't say I have."

"Well you should try it Jane, at least once, you can trust me I'm not like the property developers you normally meet. I also work as an instructor with Sussex police, observing other motorcyclists and helping them get through their tests, so I'm pretty safe on the road."

"Really, sounds interesting. I'm sure that must be rewarding." I said feeling impressed by his social conscience.

"I'll get you on a bike yet, all you have to do is trust me."

"Sure" I said, "shall we go in my car?" I wasn't about to let him think I would trust that easily.

We drove to the site and whilst we walked around, I explained the history behind it. It was one I knew very well, having played in the ruins as a child.

We were interupted momentarilly by Robert who rang on the mobile insisting we meet for a drink in a nearby pub. Alan went in first.

> "Robert's in here somewhere. What will you have to drink Jane?"
>
> "Orange juice please."
>
> "That sounds like a good idea, I'll join you. It's not good to drink during the day."
>
> "I find it makes me tired," Alan smiled, as if that was a good remark to make.

It wasn't long till we spotted Robert, who looked like he'd been there quite a while, as he was a bit on the tipsy side. I could clearly see that Alan was concerned about Robert's demeanour, so we had a quick drink and I offered to drop him home. Alan walked ahead with Robert, as my mobile had started to beep.

> "Excuse me a minute, I've just got to answer this, hello" I was shocked to hear Adrian at the other end, virtually in hysterics.
>
> "Don't trust Robert, I just had him touch me up at a bus stop!! I think he's gay and he's definitely an alcoholic."
>
> "What? Are you all right?" "Please listen to me Jane. I don't trust Robert, just take care."
>
> "Ok, thanks for your advice. Goodbye." I said, not fully knowing

how to handle the call and continued toward the car.

We dropped Robert off first, and then drove back to pick up Alan's motor bike.

> "Is something bothering you?" Alan asked "it's just, you seem a little tense after your call."
>
> "Hmm... well, you could say that, it was the town centre manager. He called to tell me Robert had molested him at a bus stop."
>
> "What?" He said looking shocked.
>
> "I know, it sounds bizarre. It's rumoured he's got a drink problem and I've tried to talk with him about it but......... ."
>
> "But why did he mention Robert?"
>
> "Beats me. It's a bit worrying though. I guess he's got to face up to the fact he's got a problem. We've all got our demons to face."

I said trying to sound positive but feeling completely confused by the call.

> "Well, he could have a point about Robert's drinking, Jane.

They say it takes one to know one. And having seen Robert today, I'm not sure I trust him or Nick. They've had some very ambitious plans and mentioned large household names with potential to make them vast amounts of money but so far nothings happened. I understand you were instrumental in helping them with some of the work?"

"Not really, I did a bit of typing and I'm a good listener that's all. If I can provide a few contact points, that benefit companies I deal with, I will. That's it really but I understand you've known Robert for a long time."

"I've known his family for sometime. I met Robert through a solicitor when he worked in London, as a Bond Trader, so I don't know him as well as you think. Hmmm I don't think you believe me" he said looking at my expression "Look lets be honest, I think it boils down to the fact that, I'd really appreciate your view of Lansdown?"

"But that's not for me to say Alan, I've known Robert for less than five minutes in comparison to you. Surely you're more informed than I? My involvement is merely one of offering marketing help and a bit of typing, and that's all! "

"But what do you think they do? Be honest Jane?"

"Well, I felt uneasy about the office set up. The equipment is dated and doesn't seem related to the kind of stock, they say they're carrying. But I haven't seen the accounts, so I don't have a clue. Maybe it's a front for something?" I said, trying to bring a little light humour to the situation.

Alan's face hardened,

"What do you mean by that -drugs?" I felt his eyes dart across my face.

"I really couldn't say", I said laughingly, wishing I'd kept my mouth shut.

I already knew Robert smoked a bit of grass. He didn't hide the fact but then so did a lot of people in South London.

"They're obviously going through a bad patch Alan, a lot of companies fail within the first 18 months. It's quite common. You haven't got anything tied up in the company have you?"

"No, I've had a few business dealings with Robert in the past, none of which ever came to anything. In fact he's caused me a considerable amount of trouble and embarrassment by not being able to deliver what he promised. So I decided some time ago not to do business with him in the future. Patrick Harding on the other hand, seems to have invested quite heavily in the company, around £70,000 I believe, and he hasn't been paid for rent either."

"Can I ask, why you continue being friends with Robert if you think so little of him and If you don't mind me asking, what's your line of work again?"

"I'm a property developer but before you say anything Jane, not all property developers are crooks. I just fell on hard times for a while. I've been very successful in my line of work and have known Robert's father for years. He just needs a taste of success again like me. He apparently met Patrick in a pub and as Patrick had the premises, which were vacant at the time and Robert had the ideas. The company was set up, giving Patrick 30% shares with a 25% split in profits on contracts that were promised, which would have brought in around £250,000 in the first 18 months of trading. Robert agreed to pay Patrick the rent for the offices, however, as you can see, things didn't go according to plan. I don't see much money going into the bank and I believe Robert and Nick are getting paid cash in hand. Robert seems quite hyper a lot of the time, as if he's on something."

"Are you trying to tell me he's taking drugs? "

"Oh, I don't know, Jane, but I smell a rat. Apparently the bank stopped funding some time ago when they went over the overdraft limit of £25,000 and they're pushing for personal guarantees from both directors. But as Robert and Nick don't have an asset to their name, the bank won't be getting much back. What do you think of that?"

"I don't see it has anything to do with me. If you have any suspicions you should go to the police." Alan looked perplexed.

"I can't do that, I don't have any proof."

"Look, as I said earlier, it's common for companies to fail within the first 18 months of trading."

I was beginning to feel I didn't need to know any more - information overload. Why was he asking me, a virtual stranger!!? He noticed my uneasiness.

"Look, I'm sorry Jane, let's change the subject. Tell me about yourself. Robert speaks highly of you, although at this moment in time, it probably doesn't help much. You work with small businesses in the area don't you?"

"Yes, that 's right, I've lived in the area for a number of years."

I told him a bit about myself and listened as he tried to reassure me of his integrity. He seemed a pleasant enough man, keen to leave me with a good impression. We arrived back to where he had left his motor bike.

"Do keep in touch Jane, there may be some business we can do together. Don't judge me based on Robert."

"Ok, I won't, I'll keep an open mind", I said.

He did seem a little out of place in Robert's company and I knew he felt sorry for him, so maybe the tie, was with Robert's father.

To me it was just a job. I met all sorts of people and one thing I had learned in life, was not to judge.

"You're not convinced Jane", Alan said as he sorted out his bike gear. "I'm going to prove to you that you can trust me. Look, would you like me to ring the town centre manager and tell him to leave you alone, I can do that for you at least. I used to have a PA who is now my best friend and I know she wouldn't take that kind of nonsense, she knows how to deal with men. She worked for me when my company collapsed and even though I couldn't pay her, she still came in. I don't forget favours, let me deal with it for you. I'll be diplomatic don't worry."

"You'd better be, remember I have to work with him"

"Of course, I'll keep that in mind, don't worry. It's been lovely meeting you, Jane and I'm interested in the site you showed me today, I work with some major property companies. St Augustin's Property Corporation is one of them. Do you know them?"

"Sorry Alan, it's not my line of work. I don't, know many property companies. I've worked mainly with IT companies."

"Can you arrange a meet with the council?"

"Yes, I'm sure I can do that. They're always interested in having further talks, especially if you've got the contacts. My understanding is that the current developer may be pulling out. So I'm sure they'd be interested."

"He looked straight into my eyes "I'm serious about this Jane, I'd be happy to pay you an introduction fee, remember."

"What, on something this big?" I laughed and he grasped my hand and for a brief moment and our eyes met, realising how stupid this must have looked, I slowly removed my hand from his grasp.

He smiled. "I'd better go."

Grace was still at work, so it was quiet for a change. No Television, no record player, just bliss. Complete silence and tranquillity. I went to my room, suddenly overcome by tiredness, I kicked off my shoes and lay on the bed, my head spinning.

Who was Alan Sedgewick and where does Robert, fit in? I assured myself it wasn't anything to do with me, and before long drifted off.

I awoke to find Grace leaning over the bed laughing.

"Sorry, I had a bit of a stressful day." I mumbled, What time is it?"

"6.00 o'clock, here's a cup of tea and what's for dinner?"

"Thanks, I haven't even thought about dinner. How was your day?"

"Really boring mum but I'm off to the cinema shortly."

"In that case I'd better prepare something quickly." I said beginning to panic.

"Thanks mum, got to go and get myself ready"

"OK. What time will you be back?"

"Cinema finishes about 11.00 so should be back about 11.30 pm at the latest. Don't worry we're getting a lift home."

"Ok but don't forget your mobile."

"I won't" And with that she went off to her room.

I got up, put on an oven ready meal and went to answer the phone.

"Hello Sam, yes, no I haven't forgotten, I'm leaving, in half an hour."

"Mum can you drop me off, Rachel has just texted me and we are meeting earlier, so don't have time to eat,"shouted Grace.

"Excuse me a minute." I said holding my hand over the receiver.

"Only if you're ready to go in the next 15 minutes. I've arranged to meet Sam this evening."

"Sorry Sam I've got to drop Grace off on the way."

I got my coat, jumped in the car and waited whilst Grace gathered her belongings and drove over to Rachel's.

"Have a nice evening, you know where I am if you need me, you've got the number"

"Thanks mum, see you later."

Sam had been through a bad relationship, one where she was ripped off for a considerable amount of money. The police were involved, after he forged her signature on documents, scary stuff. So I listened whilst she 'rubbished' men.

"But they're not all like that, Sam "

"You won't say that when it's your turn," she said.

I'd worked in a predominantly male environment most of my career and on the whole, found they were pretty straightforward and had some good male friends as a result. Sam on the other hand, started her career after her first divorce, when the children were teenagers and, understandably, was very angry about her present situation which had now been going on a number of years.

"It will happen to you one day, mark my words, Jane, you should be careful."

I smiled, "I will, but I can't think why, it's just people. We just get it wrong sometimes but you shouldn't condemn the whole male race. Look is there anything I can do to help?"

"You may be right, would you mind typing a report for the police."

"Of course, just show me what to do."

I sat at the computer and started to piece together the relevant dates and events as Sam dictated them to me:

5th Mar 1996   Nigel Watson convinced my mother (Mrs Smith) he needed £3,000 in order to purchase a company.

20th Mar 1996 I was appointed director of the new company in order to protect my mother's interests. Nigel had become close to my family and we were romantically linked. He was very persuasive about the benefits of a family business.

17th Nov 1996 Nigel convinced my brother (Andrew Smith) to invest in the business £7,000. Nigel said he would raise £10,000 himself and his father had agreed to lend him the money.

December 1996 I agreed to invest £20,000 by increasing my mortgage by this amount for the now joint business venture

8th Dec 1996 A mortgage offer was drawn up. Nigel told me he would deal with all the paperwork and enlisted the help of a friend of his Marion Henderson, from a firm of Financial Consultants.

10th Dec 1996 I Married Nigel Watson

5th Jan 1997 Mortgage was agreed based on above. At this point I thought I'd increased my mortgage to £102,000 + costs and was investing in a company venture along with my family.

25th Jan 1997 The business Homertons Residential opened on 25th Jan and I worked full-time (7days a week) at the premises in 8 Wardean Drive, SW17. For the first   6 months I did not take any form of remuneration. I became worried about the mortgage repayments, which appeared to be very high, and when I questioned Nigel about this he evaded giving me an answer.

22nd Feb 1997 As I'd been appointed a Director of Homertons, Nigel told me I could become the Company Secretary, which was a better position and Lorraine Stevens who was the present Secretary resigned.

18th Mar 1997 Nigel asked me to sign papers to resign as director insisting we only needed one director and one Company Secretary.
This was confirmed by Elizabeth Friar of Weston & Finnes, who later became our solicitors.

Sept 1997 It was decided to sell my house in Pimlico due to the high mortgage repayments and in September 1997, I found and purchased a flat in Wimbledon. From the proceeds of this sale I expected to get approx. £60,000 and was alarmed when this did not arrive.
I rang the bank who told me I had a primary account and a secondary account. I told her, I didn't know what a primary and a secondary account meant. Her answer was, she thought Nigel and I had already discussed this. So I rang the solicitors and they told me to take the chequebook away from Nigel. At this point I was very angry and told the solicitors to make sure the new flat remained in my name only, which they did. I confronted Nigel over 'the lost' monies and he told me he would pay me back from the Company. At this time the business was flourishing. Turnover 26/2/1997 to 10/10/1997 was £150,340.81.
I made an appointment to see our accountant and he advised me I should hold shares in the company and said he had been unaware of my financial input. Nigel told him the financial backing came from a rich uncle. The accountant gave me the correct forms so I could secure shareholding but Nigel refused to offer me anything, telling me, it was now his business. However, he agreed to repay me in full, if I continued working at Homertons.

January 1998 I felt I had no choice and eventually agreed. Nigel then approached my brother for a further loan of £2,500. He agreed with my brother the monies should be paid directly to a firm of solicitors (Orkins, based in Warwickshire) and this was to clear a debt with the local bank, which my brother did. My brother initially refused but Nigel was persistent telling my brother he would repay the £7,000 at the end of February and £2,500 would be repaid from the business account on the same day. My brother accompanied him to the bank and the exchange was made.

April 1998 One day in the office I saw paperwork, which indicated monies were still outstanding to our accountants.
May 1998 In a further letter dated 15/5/98 the accountants wrote to say they had been promised a bankers draft which had not been forthcoming

and indicated the funds may have been used for the 'property investment'. The property referred to in this letter, I believe to be 76 Upton Ave, London SW7. I later did a land search and found this property was in the name of a friend of Nigel's - Ross Kilban, an architect who lives in Surrey. He was originally one of our clients and we sold his property at 30 Wendover Road, London SW2.

Around this time Nigel told me he was buying a flat for investment in Bovery Road, London SW7 and asked me for my help financially. I was dumbfounded.

May 1998 Our accountants were then replaced by Norman Greendale & Co who had been recommended to Nigel by a friend of his.

At this point I saw paperwork for Tax/NI totalling £6,681.51 for the year 1997/1998 which the accountants pointed out, remained outstanding.

Nigel was by now seldom in the office or at home, and I was trying to carry on the business although it was increasingly difficult to get hold of him.

May 1998 Most alarmingly Nigel begun following me and causing problems, wherever he could. He sacked me from my job and when I refused to leave until he paid me the monies he phoned the police and further denied to the police we were married.

Strangely enough Nigel now began to offer me the business, telling me he was more interested in property development and we could work together and help each other. However, on the advice of my solicitor, I declined the offer.

November 1998 I received a letter from a firm of Insolvency Practitioners, who advised me Homertons Estates was to be liquidated.

September 2001 I was contacted by an ex-colleague, who asked if I would speak to a builder who wanted to talk with me about Nigel. The builder told me Nigel owed him £6,000, which he loaned to Nigel as a deposit on a property. This was the same property, Nigel told me about in May.

I carried out a land search, which showed Nicola James was the leasehold owner of the property. I now know this to be Nigel's new girlfriend.

October 2001 The builder P.J. Fouls recently contacted me to say Nigel sold this property, without paying him and also took a further £2,000 from the new owner on a promissory of carrying out works on the flat. This work has never been done. The owner was heavily pregnant with her second child and also has a disabled child.

Sam then dictated a statement:

> 'It's now clear to me that this was premeditated by Nigel to obtain monies from family, the business and myself by way of deception.
> He left bills including payment to the Inland Revenue and accountants in a deliberate way to allow him to take further monies from the business, which have presumably been used for other ventures. I enclose copies of documentation verifying this'.

Having completed the task, we changed the subject, I knew how much this upset her even though these events were sometime prior to us meeting. She was moving on, she was getting involved in a new business venture and wanted my advice.

"I've got it right this time Jane."

"I hope so for your sake. You deserve it."

This time she'd met a chap some 20 years her senior who wanted to back her in business.

"Would you look through these for me?" She passed me a rough draft agreement, consisting of a few scribbled notes made between them, which I read, pointing out things, she should clarify.

When we finished Sam made me a cup of tea.

"Let me do something for you. My cousin and I read tea leaves. Would you like me to read yours?"

"OK", I said laughing, "I've never had my tea leaves read before."

Sam poured the brew as we sat chatting about our families and when I had finished she turned the cup upside down and placed it in the saucer.

"Now, I'm going to read the messages in your cup" She picked it up and cradled it in her hands, looking at the formation of tea leaves.

"You should be careful Jane, I see a man approaching you. I see the possibility of great happiness but I also see you will be wrongly accused of something."

"Well that's clear then," I said. "Thanks, I'll keep an eye out for anything suspicious. Is that the time, I didn't realise it was so late, look I really should be going."

"Thanks for your help, Jane"

"No problem Sam, that's what friends are for, I'll call you tomorrow, bye."

I felt a bit relieved to get out, too much doom and gloom for one evening. I went home feeling maybe Sam was right, I should stay away from relationships for a while.

The following day I e-mailed the details to the address Alan gave me and was surprised when I got an immediate reply. 'I'll pass by tomorrow. Will you be around?'
I e-mailed back, 'will be around from 12 to 3'.
'Good, would like to go over a few things with you, see you then, Alan'

He arrived around 1.00 pm, and when I opened the door, his intense stare made me blush. I knew he'd noticed and felt angry with myself for being so foolish, being shy was a definite drawback at times. That was one of the reasons I went into sales, it allowed me to be friendly and confident and hide the weak traits in my character.
"Why don't I take you for lunch, Jane?"
I found myself trying to think of a valid reason why I shouldn't but failed miserably.
"Hmm, why not", I said, sounding like a blithering idiot.
I avoided eye contact and grabbed my coat.
"Look rather than take two cars, leave yours here and I'll drop you back later" I found myself agreeing as he opened the door for me to step inside.
The Panama hat I'd seen before lay in the back window. We drove to the same restaurant, only this time I was ravenous. After I relaxed a little, we spoke about a myriad amount of things, our thoughts on life, likes, dislikes and ideas for the future and found we had a lot in common. He was so charming, that it made me feel dizzy.
"Look I could really use a person like you in my business. But I guess, I'd better drop you back home," he said, placing his head to one side and looking as if he were reluctant to let me go.
"Thanks, I've had a wonderful lunch, but I really do need to get back."
As I got out of the car he took my hand and rubbed it gently............
"I'm so pleased we met." I felt my hand shake, as goose pimples ran up my arm.
"Can we meet again, maybe next week? Please say yes." The 'yes' slipped out before I realised what I was saying, as if it were impolite to say no.

We agreed to meet the following week and discuss a strategy, which would be mutually beneficial.

It wasn't long before this became a regular event and I found myself more and more attracted to this man. We talked incessantly covering all sorts of diverse subjects and Alan confided in me about his marriage. He had been in an anodyne relationship, devoid of love in any physical sense and had been separated for the past 10 years.

He asked about my past and was surprised when I became evasive. I explained it had been difficult and that I didn't want to talk about it.

> "Look Jane I want to know all about you. Not all men are bastards. I 'm really quite sensitive. I want a relationship with you, and only you, and I can only do that if I know all the facts. You have to trust someone in your life."

I thought about it, he was right of course, maybe he was the person I could tell my story to without worrying about reprisals.

When asked about my past, I'd say I'd been married but things just didn't work. I remember all too well, how David reacted. He had been there when I was still trying to untie myself from the business and heard the cold way I spoke with Andy, so he didn't believe me when I said Andy had been violent toward Grace and me.

'Don't ever talk to me that way, will you, Jane and if you hit me the relationship's finished. Do you understand?' I know things got verbally pretty ugly with Andy, toward the end, but as for hitting David, well it wouldn't have entered my head, why should it?

My anger was only directed back at the source.

I would try and tell people we just didn't get on but unfortunately, the next question would always be- 'do you keep in touch'. I have always been the worst possible liar. What usually came to mind was "do you really think I would keep in touch with a monster like that!!!?"

But I would bite my tongue and say, 'Grace sees him from time to time'.

I looked into Alan's eyes, should I trust him? Isn't that what men do, pretend to have a sensitive side, get you to tell them your life and then use it against you.

> "It just wasn't a pleasant experience, that's all." I said.

> "You're going to have to tell me one day" he said looking deeply into my eyes.

If I told him Andy was violent towards us, the comment that usually came back - 'you don't look like the type of person to warrant your husband hitting you'.

44

I used to get angry about those comments, you just couldn't win, if you said you did nothing wrong, you looked, weak and pathetic, if you said, you answered back, you were hot-headed. Either way, you lost.

I'd certainly never told David the whole story, he didn't want to know and it seemed such a long time ago I couldn't see the point in raking it all back up again. But Alan was persistent,

> "Jane, let me tell you what went wrong in my marriage. It was based on secrets and lies. I don't want to make that mistake again. You can understand that, can't you? If we are going to have a meaningful relationship, it has to be based on honesty and I can see from your eyes you're hiding something."

He had a way of getting what he wanted, asking small insignificant questions about my marriage, which he then began to piece together in such a way, that I felt the need to correct him.

> "It wasn't like that Alan."
>
> "How was it then? Tell me. I won't get angry, just tell me the truth."

Bit by bit I found myself answering his questions and in turn, he told me about his wife, who had many secrets and exaggerated or lied to hide things from him.

So for the first time in my life, I spoke openly about the past to someone who had been through his own adversities.

> "Look, Jane, I really believe we can help one another. I've never spoken about my past to anyone. My wife and I just avoided the subject. You tell me your life and I'll tell you mine. You and I have some uncanny similarities."

But the closer we got to each other the more frightened I became it was all too blissful, I found myself being drawn in to that warm friendly environment one I'd longed for, but never dared to think possible.

He told me he understood kids and would be happy to help with Grace, if there were any issues as he and his wife had fostered children from abused backgrounds. Eventually adopting two of their own, who he nurtured, as he worked mainly from home, which enabled him to be there whilst the children were growing up.

> "I can be a great support to Grace, she just needs a bit of understanding, that's all and more importantly she needs a normal home-life. We can do this together, it's time you felt that. You deserve some happiness."....................................

He asked me to accompany him on several business trips and was keen to tell me of his work. I protested at first, saying I wouldn't understand but he insisted.

"It won't take long for you to pick it up, Jane. All you have to do is listen to what I say. It will give us a chance to get to know each other, just say yes."

"Ok, I'll give it a try." I said nervously.

"I want to make you happy Jane," he said with gusto and leaned forward to kiss me on the lips. "Shall we meet up later, I have a few business things to deal with at the office. I'll call you around 6.30 pm. See you then"

I stood and watched him drive away, knowing he would be back in only a few short hours.

Pull yourself together, I kept telling myself, this isn't real and turned round to find Grace looking at me, strangely.

"You like him don't you?" She said.

"Yes I do, is it that obvious?"

She looked at me with a puzzled expression on her face and nodded but was willing to let me try one last time, as she put it.

The phone rang,

"Jane the deals I'm working on will allow me to make you happy. You deserve some happiness in life and it's long overdue and I'm going to make it my job to see that happens."

"Sounds great Alan, I'll go with that one," I said.

"I'm coming over later, give you a call on the way, just need to tidy up a few things here first."

He was now coming over three evenings a week, he had a way about him that made it difficult to say no and he did it with such affection that it was almost contagious.

Meanwhile, I was having problems with my computer, it was doing the strangest things. The cursor had developed a mind of its own and was beginning to slow down completely. I virus checked the software but drew a blank, drawn to the possibility of component failure, that's all I need. And then the phone rang again.

"You sound a bit down."

"Hi Alan, Oh, I've just got a problem with my computer, it's acting a bit weird"

"Why don't you throw it away and buy a new one?"

"I can't do that, it's not that old and I don't have the money to just bin it.

I'm going to persevere for a bit longer and ask for some advice."

"You shouldn't waste your time like that, its counter productive. I just throw them in the bin and get a new one, much simpler."

"You're probably right, but I don't want to give up just yet, it's either a component failure or I'm being hacked in to."

He laughed, "I'll leave you to it. I'll be over around 7.00 pm. You know what I think."

"Yes, OK, drive carefully, see you later."

I looked forward to Alan coming over and before long our relationship became physical. For the first time in my life I felt fulfilled, loved and content. I enjoyed our love-making and realised what I'd been missing. Andy had been so abusive that it wasn't something I'd ever enjoyed, it was more perfunctory or is that strictly true? As years with David, had helped that go away.

With Alan it was different, after a couple of months, he asked me to marry him. It seemed we had so much in common, that my answer, yes shocked even me when it came out. If I'm honest, it had become a bit of a whirlwind romance but it seemed so right, he was so understanding and I'd virtually given up the thought of being happy. That was for other people.

Alan was right, I needed to be pampered for a while and lapped up the attention.

I carried on with my work locally and heard that Lansdown was now about to got bust. Alan rang saying he was concerned for Robert, how he would react to being made bankrupt and whether this would push him further down the route of binge drinking.

"I know it's sad Alan but there's not much you can do. People need to admit they have a problem before they start healing."

"How did you become so wise?"

"Who knows, years of practice and learning the hard way. Catch you later."

I rushed home, having first picked up Grace and rang one of my wisest friends, Robin.

"Hi, I've met the most wonderful person."

"Really Jane? Tell me more. Is he solvent? "

"Robin, don't be so judgmental."

"Look, Jane I just want you to be happy. You deserve it but please be careful."

Robin had had his own problems with relationships and was philosophical about life. Like me he was wary and I respected his views.

"You know I encourage women to be independent, Jane."

"I know you do but I'm already independent, and now I want a soul mate, someone I can rely on and Alan's offering the chance to be a part of a family. I know you went through a bad time with relationships but he really understands me and likes Grace. He's got strong views not dissimilar to my own and has worked with abused children, so maybe one day Grace will feel comfortable talking with him about her past and maybe he can help. He's got two kids himself of similar ages"

"What Jane? Slow down, sounds a bit too perfect if you ask me! There are too many maybes. You've only known him five minutes!"

I liked Robin, he was a man in his late fifties and always gave me objective advice.

"I guess I just want it to work. I haven't given up on the human race yet."

"Jane, you're a lovely person, just don't get hurt. People say all sorts of things when they first meet."

"I know, but if I get too sceptical about life, I'll just think I deserved everything that happened to me."

He laughed "Jane", he said taking a deep breath. "You have an amazing ability to brighten anyone's day. You've certainly never spoken to me about your past, just be careful that's all. I am a bit busy right now, you've caught me in the middle of a paperwork day, catch you later?"

"Of course, bye Robin."

Robin was always difficult to get hold of. He'd been introduced through a business colleague and shyed away from relationships. He kept himself busy with one project or another, often years in the making but always determined to see them through to the end and I admired him for that.

Alan was now staying a lot during the week and when we weren't together we were constantly on the phone. He was still resolving issues with his wife, the divorce papers had been put together some months before we met, and he had moved out of the matrimonial home, to prove to me he was serious about making a new life together. At weekends I joined him at his rental, a small annexe, overlooking fields. It was here, he encouraged me to continue with my writing, whilst he went about his day to day business and it gave me a break from the piles of boxes that were mounting in my home in readiness of the move.

"Look, one of the reasons I like you Jane is that you don't judge people. You didn't know anything about me when we met

and I was worried you'd look upon me as a part of Lansdown."
I looked at him, puzzled. "I trust you sufficiently enough Jane
to tell you about my life and I want you to feel, you can do the
same."

"It would be a great relief Alan, for years I've been unable to talk
with anyone. Society doesn't want to know people like me."
He pulled me towards him and kissed me tenderly on the lips.

"I want us to be the best of friends and want you to feel you can
tell me anything, anything at all. Do you understand? I love you
Jane. I just wished we'd met years ago. I would have protected
you. You should have called me."

I laughed "That would have been nice. What's the time? Oh, no,
I have to go. It's going to take me some time to get back, I'm
picking up Grace. It's been lovely being here but now I've
got to run."
He gave me a warm smile and held me tightly.

"I don't want to let you go Jane. I want you to be with me
always. However, I appreciate Grace needs you too, so I'll let
you go and we'll speak later."
As I left I felt full of energy, wrapped in a warm feeling, that made me glow
with happiness.

Back home, I had a visit from a potential buyer for the house and Robin
kindly came round and was instrumental in helping me push the deal
through. Alan rang later, he always did. He needed to know where I was,
and that I was safe. That's one of the downsides of telling someone your
past, He was worrying about me. He didn't like London, and found it a
threatening environment to live in. Street muggings, theft, assault are
commonplace. But I've lived here all my life, it becomes a way of life. You
get used to it.

"Alan, it looks like I've got an offer on the house, which I've
accepted, fantastic isn't it?"
"Great, where are you going to move to?"
"Oh, I don't know. One step at a time. This isn't the first time this
chap has put in an offer and then retracted it."
"Well, I want you to move nearer to me, where I can look after
you."
"That's a lovely thought but I don't know anything about the
property prices down there and it's a long way from family
and friends."
"You would only be an hours drive away and my children would
love you, you know how worried I am about them. I'm worried
Mandy will do something to harm them, she's not taking this

divorce at all well. Can I bring Lucy up to stay? I'm sure you two would get on well."

"Of course, I would love to meet her, she could stay over but won't that cause a problem with Mandy?"

"No, of course not I've been quite open about everything"

I felt quite honoured that he would bring his daughter to stay and reassured that Mandy and he were trying to deal with their divorce reasonably.

"Ok, I'll ask, let's speak later. I'll come over this evening, if that's all right. I'm finding this all a bit too difficult, Mandy is being difficult over a few things and I'd love to see you."

"Of course, look forward to it. I'll cook dinner. Shall we say 7.00 pm?"

"I'll give you a ring when I am leaving, bye my love."

"Bye, darling."

He loved to visit when he had a stressful day or there was an important case going on. Apart from his property dealings, he was also a surveyor undertaking difficult cases for local builders.

Mandy was involving the children too much, which upset him greatly, and although they were old enough to understand, it was still wrong but easilly done.

When we were together it was like a couple of teenagers, laughing and giggling, almost effervescent, I couldn't have been happier. It was as if, at long last, I'd found the soul mate I'd always wanted. Someone I could talk to, bounce ideas off, who loved and respected me.

It didn't take long, till the contracts for the house sale were in place, although, I had to agree a deadline, or risk losing the sale. As the deadline approached, I was suddenly aware I would be out with nowhere to go. Having run a business from home I was left with the residue, the mess that no one wanted, the clutter of component parts of no use to anybody and I probably didn't recognise it at the time but I was physically exhausted.

Grace stayed at Mum's, whilst our possessions were placed in storage and I started the arduous task of looking for suitable property.

In the meantime Alan let me move in to his rental and continued encouraging me to pull the jumble of notes together in the form of a manuscript, although much of this was already done, the biggest problem I had, was what was I going to do with it. I toyed with the idea that this could be a project we could do together, as I needed a male perspective. In the meantime, I registered with a few estate agents in the surrounding areas, Alan was insistent I move nearer to him and for the first time ever, I would rid myself of a mortgage. The countryside was lovely and it sounded an attractive proposition, although the move had brought me close to a nervous breakdown. My back being the worst problem, I had worked myself too hard and now had trouble walking.

"I bet that has never happened to you before, has it Jane? You won't need to worry about working for a while and in a year's time, I'll have enough to provide for both of us."

It sounded lovely but I knew this was the beginning of our relationship and these were just the words of two people emotionally tied up with one another and very much in love. They say love is blind but we all need to jump in to test the waters from time to time.

We had a few ups and downs, Alan read part of my notes and was critical of my past, so I decided not to let him read anymore, when the words came out of his mouth 'you deserved it'. That was my first disappointment but I had been told you had to have the experience to understand it.

"I am a predatory character you know, Jane"

"That's a funny thing to say, what do you mean?"

"Don't you worry. Look, let me come round and view some property with you. I'm sure we can find somewhere nice"

Moving around was difficult, so I was pleased Alan wanted to help. I noticed he was showing signs of stress himself and at times took his frustration out on me. However, the good times outweighed the bad and we went for little 'holidayettes' as he described them to recuperate.

With Alan's help, I found a lovely 4 bed-roomed cottage, moved in and for the first month everything was wonderful. I continued editing the manuscript, the notes began to flow, turning from paragraphs, to chapters. The cathartic exercise I started some years ago was exhilarating. It felt I was letting go and finally being allowed to move on.

There was still, a lot to do on the home front. All my belongings arrived en masse and I was suddenly overwhelmed with boxes.

Alan spent time popping back and forth, to his rental and his matrimonial home, where his ex-wife, unbeknown to me, was also in the process of moving. As soon as one box was emptied he took them for her to use. I comforted myself with the thought, that at least they are still talking. He also had the gruelling task of collecting his belongings, some of which went directly to his rental and some to the cottage.

My work was put on hold, whilst I tried to assemble some sort of order in our new abode.

Eventually Alan moved in.

"Look we have been through a lot, so how would you like to go on holiday for a week in the sun, we could do with a break Jane, what do you think?" I didn't need much persuading.

"I'd love too. It sounds just the tonic we both need."

Alan made the arrangements, booking a villa in Lanzarotte, through a friend of his Michelle, a travel agent, who I hadn't yet met. The villa was fine, except Alan was constantly on the phone and then there was that fateful night. We'd been out for a meal and were making our way back to the villa when two men crossed the road and brushed in front of us. Alan was carrying my handbag over his shoulder, having just convinced me, I needn't worry about anything anymore as he was going to look after me. But shortly after he spoke the words, I felt a sudden chill go down my spine and stupidly fought with the feeling for a moment before acting.

"Move over here", I said forcing him toward a shop window, away from what I felt was impending danger.

Two young men ran at us, grabbing the bag and causing Alan to spin round and fall. They darted up an alley, and not knowing what to do I followed. It opened into a cul-de-sac, where I saw both men jump over a garden wall and start chatting with a man that came from the house, as if to greet them.

"Jane, Jane, get back here"

I was striding towards the house, when I heard Alan's voice and turned to see his face. He was angry.

"Come back now." He demanded.

Instinctively I walked over to him and he hurried me away.

"We'll phone the Civil Guard, Jane."

Everything we had was in the bag, passports, money, jewellery, mobile phones. It seemed ages before the Civil Guard arrived and even longer to sort things out. But they did recommend an hotel, although neither of us could sleep. Alan then upset Mandy by calling her at 1.00am on the eve of her birthday, getting her to cancel his credit cards, and forgetting to wish her happy birthday.

The following mornning he was enraged, leaving me in the hotel, whist he went to a local bar, near to the mugging to offer a reward.

"I'll get them, you'll see, no one does that to me and gets away with it."

It seemed almost laughable now, we had so many other things to sort out but I let him go and when he returned, he seemed more relaxed.

"A friend, Michelle organised this trip for us, Jane, she'd be really upset if she knew what happened. I have already contacted her and she is sending a representative to meet us at the Police station. It's amazing how you knew those young men were coming up behind us. How did you know that?"

"It's instinct. You've been trying so hard to get me to relax since we got here but I can always tell when something's wrong. Women's intuition, I guess."

Alan smiled and nodded his head,

"Women seem to have that. Mandy had it too."

The tour operator met us at the police station. She looked like she'd been up all night, her hair was greasy, her eyes deep set in their sockets, so much so that she seemed out of place, especially as we were just a short distance from the beach with the sound of the sea, and seagulls overhead. She told us she was English, having married a man from the Island and was used to this kind of thing, as it happened a lot especially to tourists. She pointed out that the Civil Guard weren't going to be much help and that all she could do was help translate so we could fill the forms in correctly.

It sullied the holiday from there, we'd only been in the villa a couple of days and now all we wanted to do was go home, or at least I did. Alan had become irritable with me, it was as if his male ego had been attacked and I was the nearest thing at hand to vent his anger.

It wasn't the same after that, both of us were 'tetchy' with one another. Alan wired some money over via Western Union and carried on making endless calls, but the following evening we slept in separate rooms, I can't really remember what the argument was about, but in Alan's eyes it was my fault. and although we tried to enjoy the remainder of our stay, it wasn't the same.

However, our relationship was still young, still vibrant but I was relieved to set foot back on British soil.

Grace joined us a month later, I didn't want to force her to move, allowing her instead to choose whether or not she stayed with friends or family. And would have been happy to support her until she was financially independent. Secretly, I was pleased when she finally made up her mind and felt sure she would settle in and make friends easily.

"I've got some important cases on at the moment and by the end of the year I'm not only free to marry but I'll be able to contribute financially. It's easy being with you Jane, you have a cute smile, which I will treasure always. You don't know what it's like being with someone who has real emotions. You make me realise just how much I missed out on over the years and the chemistry between us is so strong. It's like we were meant for each other. I'm so pleased we met." He always had a way of making me feel completely loved and it was at these times that I knew this was the man

I wanted to spend the rest of my life with.

> "If you dig out your insurance details, I'll get a chap, recommended by my accountant to chase things up for us. Is your house covered in the event of fire? I just want you to check and don't forget to see that you have buildings cover too. We will send a copy to this chap and he will deal with it.
>
> We don't need to deal with this stuff anymore, I'll get someone to do it for us. How does that sound Jane, I bet that's never happened to you before?"
>
> "What do you mean, fire?" I said completely confused.
>
> "Just look at your policy and check you're adequately covered that's all and make sure you've got the building covered."
>
> "Look, I'm covered, don't worry, so much." I said laughingly.
>
> "OK, you need to send a copy to this chap and he'll check to see if you can make a claim on the losses in Lanzarote. Ah, you look tired, why don't you go and have a lie down. You can dig the things out later."
>
> "Do I?" I said
>
> "Yes you're really not yourself, you need sleep. I can deal with these things, you don't need to worry about a thing, so off you go."

What he didn't know was that I was grappling with emotions I hadn't felt before and the soreness I'd felt in my chest for many years was beginning to heal. Time passed quickly, it's been 3 months since the move. Having reached an amicable financial settlement, with his ex-wife, allowing them both to start planning their future, it also meant we could start planning ours. Once he had received the money from his divorce he was to give me half of the value of the house. As we both wanted to start with a 'clean slate'. I had an outstanding matter pertaining to my own divorce some years ago, so Alan, Grace and I went to see the solicitor but after discussing their fees, I was still no further forward.

We returned home, whereupon Alan e-mailed them on my behalf, having set up an e-mail account in my name. Although the banter between them was a little heated, everything seemed fine, except when they didn't receive the cheque and they sent a county court summons to my old address, meaning that by the time I received it, I already had a judgement against me. They knew of the new address and a redirection was in place but I didn't receive the summons in time to do anything about it. The cheque in question had already been posted and even confirmed as being received, but as it hadn't cleared their bank account, they felt justified in their actions. It reminded me of the time when I was going through my divorce, I couldn't face dealing with anything related to

54

it because I couldn't cope with the stress, and without fail, the solicitors kept sending in their account.

Brilliant, just what I needed, having spent years trying to keep a clean slate, I've now got a blotch on my credit rating, which means I can't get credit should I need it. For some unknown reason, Alan thought I blamed him, one thing led to another and rows ensued.

The truth was I found anything connected with my divorce case a complete drain and Alan; instead of being sympathetic just got more and more angry. I tried to see things from his point of view, putting it down to the strain of his own divorce and workload but my move hadn't been an easy one and three months on, I was still finding it difficult to walk freely. Determined to keep moving, each day I got up and unpacked yet another box.

However, Alan was now dwelling on the past, reflecting on his life, his family and resenting the fact he'd moved out of his home, where he had lived with his wife some 25 years, I couldn't blame him. But contrary to what I thought had been an amicable divorce, he was angry about the way his wife had dealt with it and she was angry with him.

> "That's just the way women operate. She was fine when I was leaving, we were the best of friends. Now she wants to get back at me. I was chatting to a women friend of mine the other day and she told me, that's just the way women are. You are all like that." He said, giving me a sideways glance.

Typically, not able to confront his wife, he directed his anger at me. Asking more and more probing questions of my past, and going over and over it again, as if there were some dark secret yet to be unveiled. As for me, it was threw me back to a place I no longer wanted to revisit.

Worst of all, Grace was showing signs of stress, she had open sores on her face as the probing questions turned to arguments, which she could hear, wanting to know why I was being treated in that way.

> "I hate lies. My wife kept secrets." Alan told me. "I want a relationship based on honesty. I need to know everything about you and your past, if I'm going to understand you and Grace. I don't want to make the mistakes I made in my marriage. I typed up some notes about Mandy when we first met. She suffered from low self-esteem due to her past. I was the only one who encouraged her. Her mother died when she was young. Mandy was so upset, it's no wonder she was cold at times. I knew we weren't right for each other then, I was going

through a difficult time myself, my mum had just died, so I guess we were thrown together. We were very young, but we got married, wanted children and fostered a few kids first, some of them had been abused, so I understand kids really well. Eventually we adopted two of our own."

The story seemed unreal and I found myself drawn closer to Alan as I felt his pain and was touched by his devotion to Mandy.

We talked into the early hours as he tried to understand my life. However, rather than easing the situation, it ended with Alan attacking me, telling me I couldn't possibly understand him because I didn't know what a normal life was and unfortunately for me, this was a position I couldn't defend.

I later realised Grace probably overheard most of our talks, as she stayed in her room, refusing to get up. She was showing a range of emotions but try as I might to explain this was just a stressful time for Alan, she remained unconvinced.

As discussions turned into heated arguments, she reverted to that small child unable to do anything about her surroundings. The pain I felt was unimaginable and I directed my anger back at Alan, surely he could see what was happening and then directly at Grace as it was the only way of bringing her back to her senses.

"Get up, don't let them win, this isn't you, please you're worth more than that. If you crumble now then everything we've worked through was for nothing. We're out of that now so don't give up, you must try, Please Grace. Alan's fostered abused children, maybe he will understand where others haven't." Grace took the bait and started attacking me. "I hate you," she screamed.

"I know. Now start showing everyone you can get yourself organised. Hate me all you like. I am always going to be here for you and will always love you."

"I don't want anything to do with you. You always get it wrong, I want to be as far away from you as possible."

"Ok, do that, because the last thing I want for you, is to go through anymore pain but talk to me when you decide, promise?"

Grace agreed to talk when she decided what to do and I promised to help if she decided to return to London.

When I saw Alan later I tried to explain the difficulties I was having with Grace.

"Alan, Grace is finding it extremely difficult to settle here. We seem to be discussing a whole range of things but all she hears are rows. I need to get fit and start motivating her somehow."

"Maybe she just needs some space. Have you thought of that? We need to talk things through, if I am to understand, so why don't we go away for a few days. It can't be easy for her having a complete stranger around. She'll be fine, you worry about her too much and I'm more worried about you, so why don't I book a few days in France, we'll take the motorbike."

Alan was never one to take no for an answer and made the arrangements, assuring me it would give Grace some breathing space, where she could talk freely with friends and family and decide what was best for her. But I was beginning to realise Alan had issues of his own and Grace had been through enough but I agreed if only to allow Grace the freedom to decide.

Things were fine until we arrived in Hornfleur, having booked into the hotel he began questioning me about my life and if I tried to say, can't we just leave it, he would accuse me of hiding something or being abusive. It was as if he was analysing just so he could criticise and his voice just got louder and louder, eventually his words seemed blurred.

"Why don't you admit it" he screamed. "You'll feel better when the truth is out." On and on he went until I could hear no more, the words floated around my head and a mist descended, I placed my fingers in my ears, and yelled

"I DON'T WANT TO HEAR ANYMORE **** YOU." Confused that my own outburst had little affect, I grabbed a pillow from the bed,shouting "I'M GOING TO SLEEP IN THE BATHROOM, JUST LEAVE ME ALONE. Please Alan, just leave me alone." I was tired from the journey but Alan couldn't stop, and kept walking in, continuing to accuse me of being an abuser. "You would like that wouldn't you, for me to leave you alone, well someone's got to do something about you."

"Alan I told you I didn't want to hear anymore. I want to leave. I'll find another hotel in the morning. JUST LEAVE ME ALONE."

"No, you won't, you're not going anywhere, I won't let you. I've locked the door, we are going to thrash this out."

"Then stop shouting at me you're frightening me." I said as the tears welled up in my eyes and I fought to stop them coming out.

"The truth hurts, doesn't it and you can forget about those crocodile tears they don't work with me."

"SHUT THE **** UP, you don't know what you're talking about."

"I bet your husband taught you to speak like that, or maybe you're just a 'slapper' from South London, because you certainly talk like one."

He walked into the bedroom and as he did so, I locked the door behind him and opened the window, to get some fresh air, fanning my face to dry my tears.

I'd already collected my belongings and sat on the floor contemplating my next move. The drop from the window was too high and I felt trapped, that was always a bad thing for me, I couldn't stand being trapped with an aggressor and that was the way I was beginning to view Alan.

He continued shouting, demanding I open the door immediately, saying he was phoning the counsellor and the police to have a doctor certify me. Bemused at the thought of the counsellor and police arriving, I opened the door, thinking he was joking and would apologise but when I saw his face, I realised he meant every word.

As I tried to close it again, he wedged his foot in the gap, forcing it open, so I pushed him backwards.

"I KNEW YOU WERE VIOLENT, THAT PROVES IT. IT WAS YOU THAT ATTACKED YOUR HUSBAND, I BET HE'S GOT SOME STORIES TO TELL."

"THEN RING HIM ALAN, YOU'D PROBABLY BE THE BEST OF BUDDIES. NOW JUST GO AWAY!!!" I said sinking down onto the bathroom floor.

He continued shouting, telling me I was mad and how he would get me locked away as I had now hit him, which was proof of a violent past. He said I deserved everything that had happened to me and that the authorities back home and counsellor believed him. I could feel my head spinning and started to laugh and cry at the same time. Why had I been so stupid to tell any man my story.

"Just leave me alone Alan, go to sleep. I'll find another hotel tomorrow and we can go our separate ways. Pleeease just leave me alone."

"You're not well Jane and I am going to get help."

Silence prevailed as I sat down on the cold tiled floor, pillow wedged under my back praying for daylight. In my own mind I knew I wasn't an abuser but I did carry guilt about the past. However, I didn't have time to reflect for long, the next thing I heard was a cracking sound as he kicked open the door breaking the lock.

I felt the blood rush around my body and started to sweat profusely and feel physically sick.

He was still yelling, saying I should get up and go to bed and how pathetic I looked and at the same time took pictures on the digital camera I bought him for his birthday, saying he could show them to people when he got back.

"Please give me the keys, Alan, I just want to get out of here."

"You should be locked away, you're a danger to society. The counsellor agrees and these pictures prove you're mad.I'm sick of fending off your constant abuse."

"It's not me that's abusive but you! Can't you see that Alan?"

"I've done a lot for you and your bloody daughter. You should be grateful no-one else would put up with it. You'll never have a proper relationship with anyone because no-one will have you. I can't believe you have the audacity to accuse me of being an abuser when I've come from a normal home, one you're incapable of understanding. I've never experienced such arrogance and hypocrisy. You're pathetic Jane, just look at you."

Alan forced me into the bedroom returning to the bathroom to start repairing the lock.

"Now just get in the bed, I won't touch you. Don't worry. I have no intention of touching you. You make me sick."

I did as he asked but couldn't sleep, I started shaking as if I had been here before.

We arose around midday and booked out of the hotel, I felt totally alone and as he stomped around, I meekly followed. We'd come all this way on the motorbike and I'd given up on the thought of getting back in one piece. He told me of the powerful people he knew, saying that no-one would listen to me because of my past, and I began to believe it was true.

"You see Jane, you've been so badly damaged you didn't notice and you've damaged Grace as a result. You're lucky I'm here to help but first you have to recognise it's you. Now I came here to have a nice time. Don't worry, I'll be there to support you."

The following days passed with Alan taking on the role of the 'saviour of my life' but deep down I wanted to get home and see my daughter once again.

When we got back it was as if Grace had given up, yet more evidence to rally his beliefs that we were both mad. Seeing Grace reduced to a shell of her former self, I lost faith in everything and everyone. Alan was smoking cannabis, which he obtained from Robert and I joined him.

And this time in my life I actively encouraged Grace to leave, suggesting she got as far away from me as possible and get a flat in London with a friend. I contacted a few Youth centres to see if she could get cheap accommodation, if I couldn't get myself out of this cycle then I would find an escape route for Grace.

don't
"Grace please don't end up like me, start living your life and follow my route. I don't want to see this happen to you. You're worth so much more and don't let anyone tell you otherwise. Don't let him win. You've got to get on with your life. Remember the motivation tapes I gave you, remember the times when I kept yelling at you to get up, you've just got to do it one more time. Look in the mirror and love who you see." I said prophetically.

Days and nights seemed to roll into one and then one day, Grace waited for Alan to go out.

"I'm old enough to do something about it this Mum", she said, defiantly and I realised Grace was taking on the fight, but what for? And against whom and did anyone really want to know?

"Look, I'll have another word with Alan", I said.

Suddenly the people I cared for were all at odds with each other and there didn't seem to be anything I could do, as no one was prepared to listen. I didn't want Grace to be caught up in this, I'd already asked Alan to leave but he just wouldn't go.

When I tried again, we had yet another row where I ended up sleeping on the couch. However, the following morning he arose as if nothing had happened and instead asked my advice on his wife's new male friend, which surprised me but when I tried to ask questions, he started yelling.

"I won't take advice from you", he said sneeringly. "Someone of your calibre. My wife is nothing like YOU, she's a lady!"

He had learnt a lot from me, which seemed to explained why Mandy had chosen to lie to him during their marriage because he certainly appeared to get a sense of enjoyment out of hurting me, treating me like a small child one minute without an opinion of my own and an adult the next totally responsible for my past.

"My wife would never go out with a greasy foreigner like you, let alone marry one! You brought this upon yourself. Look at you, you've been smoking again. You're just on a self destruct because you're in denial." We stared at each other for a moment, then I left the room.

My ex had lived in this country since he was eighteen years old and I've never felt I could defend his abusive behaviour but had tried to rationalise it. It was likely he had been abused as a child and even sexually abused as a young person but that was none of anybody's business and certainly not Alan's. The day went quickly but by 6.00 am I still couldn't sleep, and went for a drive. Was I really such a bad person,maybe I could have done more, especially for Grace.

I watched as the sun rose through the clouds and the mist gently dispersed. The countryside was indeed beautiful. The air was crisp, completely different from London and had almost had a soothing affect, so I took a deep breath and watched as the mist drifted across the open fields. It was glorious. Driving always helped me think, it cleared my head. Some would say it's like running away but I enjoyed driving, it helped me focus and as for running away, well there's always a point when you have to go back and this was my home now, so there was no where to run. I stopped the car, birds were singing and rabbits darted across the fields, nibbling at the blades of grass, their ears constantly twitching, listening for danger. I smiled to myself, as I stared at the misty world unfolding in front of me, watching the rays of sun permeating through the clouds. The world's, not such a bad place after all.

I started the engine and drove the short distance back to the house and as I neared I saw Alan driving into the driveway. My heart sank, I could see in his face, he was fuming.

"I've notified the police, I've told them there's a SICK woman driving around in need of help. You should go for therapy. You definitely suffer from a SPLIT PERSONALITY!!"

I gave a half smile as I felt the pain directed at me from his anger. Well, now I have another label, I thought as I looked at him wearily.

"I would be happy to see someone, if you think it would help."

"Its not you it's GRACE. Can't you SEE the way she's controlling OUR LIVES!!"

"Really" I said feeling completely overwhelmed and wondered why he needed to bring Grace into the equation, wasn't it me he had a problem with?.

"Look", I said "Grace may have some residual affects from her past that's understandable but she's facing them and they're mainly based on trust. The arguments we're having don't help matters, she didn't want to move here in the first place, it's too remote, she's got no friends around her, she hasn't passed her driving test, so it's difficult for her to get around. The buses only run every hour and the nearest train station is 4 miles away!"

"You're always making excuses for her Jane. Other children

have no such problems. You're just avoiding what you know to be true but can't face it."

I looked at him in total disbelief and could feel another headache looming and it was only 9.O'clock in the morning.

"I really do feel quite tired. Alan, please remember my marriage was over some years ago. I wrote about it remember? And the arguments of late aren't helping."

"OK, Jane you might be right, she just needs a normal environment and I'm here to help."

"Thanks, I'm going to get some sleep now, I'm very tired." And with that I made my way to the bedroom, where I fell into a deep sleep.

It was arranged for Grace's best friend Jade to stay at the weekend, but no sooner had I woken Alan was again accusing me of doing too much for her. I reiterated the move from London had not been an easy one and I was happy to drive her around and help her get a job here. if that was what she wanted.

Grace was pleased to see Jade and everything seemed fine, except Alan's initial dislike of her. She is a typical young person, who having grown up in London, had already experienced adversity of her own, being an unfortunate witness to a drug land retaliation attack, whereby one of their members, stepped out of line and was promptly knee-capped. Too frightened to come forward and give a statement to the authorities she was understandably, wary of people. Grace and Jade had known each other since they were five years old and I knew their friendship could withstand most things. However, on Sunday morning Alan threw a paddy, accusing Grace and Jade of being 'useless so and so's'. Jade, having overheard, stayed in her room.

"You're going to be stuck with Grace till you're 75 Jane. I hoped you were more intelligent but it's obvious you've been deeply affected by your past!"

I said nothing and sat on the bed as he went red in the face and tore at a piece of paper, throwing it on the ground and stamping on it like a small child having a temper tantrum.

We'd previously agreed to drop the girls into town, but now he was asking me to make a choice, between them or him.

"Look Jane, if they're not ready to go out, they should be left behind. I'll wait in the car for 5 minutes" and with that he stormed off, staying for a few moments, before driving away.

Both girls were a bit shocked but I told them not to worry. It was a hot day after all,so I suggested they may prefer to sunbathe in the garden. I knew they had a lot of catching up to do. Alan returned a short while later and wanted to explain his behaviour, asking me to accompany him for a drive, to which I agreed, if only to get him away from the house and give the girls some time alone.

"What's the matter Alan?" I probed.

"I've told you before, I've spent 18 years with a woman who had no emotions and I don't want to get involved with more problems."

"Well, I can understand that. You've just come out of a relationship, which hurt you."

He nodded and took a deep breath.

"You think you know someone and then you're proved wrong, time and time again." He put his head in his hands and when he raised it I could see the anger in his eyes.

"You've no idea what it's been like. She knocked my confidence and ridiculed my business acumen. It's women who are the abusers in relationships. Men just put up with it." he said nodding.

"Please don't look at it that way Alan, it's just people. We're all different."

"If Grace doesn't get herself sorted with a job you'll still be paying for her when she's in her forties." He said shaking his head.

"Don't you see Jane, you're already a married couple, it's probably too late, yes I'm sure its too late."

"Grace will sort herself out. She suffering from depression at the moment." I wanted to say who could blame her and look what you're doing but I didn't see the point. He wasn't ready to listen.

It was obvious Grace was spending a lot of time in her room, which Alan took to be, a result of her disturbed past. GRACE ON THE OTHER HAND WAS ANGRY ABOUT THE MOVE, DESCRIBING OUR RELATIONSHIP AS ONE OF A WAR ZONE.

Alan was angry about his divorce, angry with his ex-wife, Grace, and angry with me, convincing himself I had a seedy past, of which, I hadn't told him the whole truth and blaming me that he had left his wife.

"You will never get better Jane until you admit who you are"............................... I heard the words but had already slipped into my world, dwelling on my own thoughts........................ WAR ZONE ....Fantastic, I moved all this way only to get my past used against me as a weapon and he's just bought in the heavy artillery. I'm smoking heavily. Cigarette after cigarette and can't and seem unable to stop. It was like letting someone into your head and then having your brains kicked in. Why was I so foolish to believe someone could possibly understand and why couldn't he just leave it at that - past? All my dreams have been dashed.

Grace had had a fit of depression once before when things at school had gone wrong for her. She wasn't good at coping with stress and locking herself away was her way of dealing with it.

We drove back to the house, where I went over to my laptop which had become my friend and confidant...

All I wanted was to be cherished and respected by someone who truly loves me for me. Isn't that what everyone wants?

Alan walked over and stared at me.

> "Look", I said turning to him "I'm going to do something constructive."

> "What's that, carry on with that pathetic book of yours."

> "Yes" I said, realising there was no point in continuing the conversation.

Alan snarled at me and walked towards the garage. What he didn't know was that I'd finished the book sometime ago and typing was now just a vehicle to rid my frustrations, because I didn't want to keep this stuff inside me.

I stared at the screen and typed..... One day I hope I can speak to someone who will understand because I can't accept this as normal. I would rather kill myself. I feel I'm being crucified for things beyond my control. I stopped for a moment deciding to do something positive and rang the police to find out if Alan, had indeed contacted them on the day I went for a drive. They told me there had been no such call and advised me to start noting things down. Strange, I thought, and then went back to the laptop, taking their advice, after all there was nothing the police could do.

I started reading through my notes and was horrified to read the childlike prose that lay before me. It was as if I'd lost the ability to write. It read like a monologue, nothing more than a series of events with no detail. I lit another cigarette and took a deep breath. My hands were shaking and tears rolled down my face and no matter how hard I tried I couldn't keep them in. I felt like I was falling apart and there was no where to turn.

The world I'd tried so desperately to get away from was closing in around me, I was trapped, totally alone and there seemed little I could do to stop what was happening. I turned off the computer and lay down on the bed. My body ached, my back was getting worse and I was tired, so tired that I could sleep forever..

I must have drifted off, because the sun was going down when I woke, and the house seemed strangely tranquil. The last rays shone faintly through the window, bouncing off a crystal windchime I had placed there, forming a rainbow on the wall. No-one was speaking, we'd reached a 'Mexican stand-off '.

Later that evening Alan tried to continue where he'd left off.

> "You know Grace has the same genes as Andy, don't you? If, she continues living with us, she's going to attack us. I can't ask my family or friends round as a result."

> I looked at him, "but that 's ridiculous! After all she's been through, that's the last thing on her mind!"

He didn't answer, instead walked down to the office we'd put together for him to work and started making private telephone calls.

I went back to the bedroom, another headache looming. Alan returned

> "Grace's got a vicious streak and she plays mind games."

> "Oh, please stop thinking like that, she's not like that ." I remonstrated.

> "You're too close, Jane; you wouldn't see it anyway, why should you, she's your child and as you've been abused most of your adult life, you wouldn't recognise it.

> You're just not used to a normal environment. The world I come from is very different from yours.

> I feel the need to lock the bedroom door at night because she worries me so much. You just don't want to see it do you Jane."

> "See what?" I said beginning to feel angered by his comments.

> "I've just been on the phone to the Samaritans." He said.

> "What? What is it with you Alan; why have you got to look for the worst in people? Analyse and criticise, isn't that what you do? Grace isn't violent. Angry maybe and who can blame her."

> "You'll never see it, Jane, you're too badly damaged. I know that now."

> "Me!!!!! Look to your own past for some answers Alan before it's too late."

> "What do you mean by that? I told you about my dad, but that was years ago and it was an accident Jane you know that."

We carried on talking into the early hours but his attitude was becoming one of indifference and anything I said just reaffirmed his analysis of the situation. Eventually he fell asleep as I lay staring at the ceiling. What had I done to deserve this? Surely enough was enough. Grace just needed to be spoken to in a normal manner, not accused of things she hadn't done!?

It must be a control mechanism to convince us all to stay in place so that none of us move on. Eventually overcome by tiredness, I fell asleep.

I awoke to find Alan standing over the bed.

"Do you know this mobile number?"

"What?, no, oh I don't know" I answered trying to gather my thoughts, having woken from a deep sleep.

"Someone rang and asked if you were here. Look at the number Jane. Speak to them, look I've just dialled the number. Here you go." He tried to thrust the phone into my hands.

"But I can't speak with someone just like that!!." I protested. I'm not even awake!!"

A man's voice answered at the other end and I made a feeble excuse and terminated the call.

"Whoever it was, was a weirdo. Kept asking for you and wouldn't give a name. You've got some funny friends Jane."

He walked off and I fell back on the bed trying to understand what had just happened. He returned a short while later

"The police are on the phone and want to talk with you."

Oh, pleeeeease, I thought, no more but he handed me the receiver. I was beginning to feel sick and in need of a cigarette.

"Hello." I said trying to sound awake.

"Are you all right madam, we just had a call from a man who says he knows you." They gave me the name and I confirmed it was an ex-work colleague.

"Are you sure you're alright? Your friend is concerned about you?" they continued.

"Yeah, I'm fine. I just woke up. I don't really know what

happened. I've got to talk with Alan about it." I put the phone down and got dressed, lighting a cigarette, and could now hear someone knocking at the door, a police car stood in the driveway. I could hear Alan chatting with the officer. Well that's it, I thought, he's finally convinced them to take me away. Alan came into the room and told me the officer wanted a word.

"What? Why?" I said trying not to sound concerned as tears rolled down my face. He muttered something inaudible and went down to the study. I followed to find a police officer waiting for me.

"Are you alright madam."

"Yes, I just had a phone call from the police, so why are you here?"

"You did. Can I speak with you in private, shall we go outside to the garden? I've just been speaking with you partner. and now I would like a word with you, if thats OK" I did as he wished and followed him outside.

"You look a bit upset madam, is something troubling you?" he said.

"I'm just tired that's all" and took another drag from the cigarette I had just lit.

"We've had a call from Christopher Hardy, do you know this man?"

"Yes," I said totally confused.

"He rang us after having a conversation with your partner. He's concerned about you. Can I ask how you know Christopher Hardy?"

"We worked together a couple of years ago and he got me some work with a company he now works for, on a contract basis but what's this all about?" I asked.

"I'm sorry, but I have to ask. Have you ever had an affair with this man."

"No, it's purely platonic. Christopher doesn't even know where I live. He's just got the phone number. He's someone I've worked with in the past and we're friends and as I was moving I gave him my number. He's someone I have known for years."

Somehow I was beginning to feel grateful for his call, but at the same time, panicking about how Alan was going to react when the officer left.

"We take these things seriously here. Physiological abuse is a crime and you look pretty stressed out to me."

Physiological abuse, a crime? What did all this mean? I thought, as I tried to gather my thoughts

"We've been having a few arguments of late but I'm sure we'll sort them out" I said.

"Are there any children in the house madam?"

"Yes, my daughter, but she's an adult." I said as I began shaking again.

"I'd like to see her anyway."

"Of course, I'll show you where she is."

The officer followed me to find Grace, who had taken refuge in the bathroom. After getting her to agree to open the door, I left him to talk with her alone. It was bizarre, we're now all in separate rooms of the house. Satisfied no-one was hurt, the officer went back to talk with Alan then left, followed shortly afterwards by Alan, who just glared at me.

The following day Alan called and asked me to accompany him for lunch to talk things over, saying he realised I hadn't involved the police and whilst we were eating he took a call on his mobile.

> "Can't talk right now, I have someone with me." I was now, just someone and he seemed embarrased by the call.
> "Sorry about that, it's very rude of me." He turned away and started staring with a fixed glaze.
> "I know you don't trust people and I want you to know everything I do, so that you know I haven't lied. This will give us a stronger relationship."

However, lunch continued in virtual silence. So much for the stronger relationship, I thought.

> "Your mood has changed again. I can see that split personality coming through, Jane" He said shaking his head, half-smiling.

"You know it's there, don't you?"

I realised we were back on labelling again.

> "Shall we go", I suggested, feeling bored with the subject. He looked at me coldly, got up from his seat and strode off ahead, turning from time to time to stare at me through gritted teeth. He was getting angry again, shaking his head, as if he couldn't understand why I wasn't keeping up.

> "Why do you insist on having mood swings Jane." He yelled.

> "It's not me Alan, it's you." But he didn't listen, instead continued accusing me of having a split personality and asking why I wouldn't admit to it. By now we'd reached the car, however he still insisted I should admit to my 'other self'.

> "The police know it's you, they're asking me if there's any mental instability in your family and they're right aren't they? The hell you must have put your previous partners through, you should be made to pay. You can't go around treating people like this. The police officer that came round also asked if Grace had the mental age of a fifteen year old."

His face was red, with anger and sweat was pouring from his brow. We got into the car and he drove off at speed.

> "Please stop the car Alan." I said feeling sick but he growled and kept driving "If you don't stop the car, I'm just going to get out"

"YOU'RE MAD", he screamed"

"THEN STOP THE ******* CAR!!" I yelled back. Eventually he pulled over, and I got out. I needed some fresh air and sat by the roadside to light yet another cigarette.

"I've got friends you know and you've got some serious problems." He said, as he texted someone on his mobile phone. No one messes with me."

When I'd finished I got back into the car and we drove the rest of the way in silence.

We arrived at the house

"You know you've just tried to jump out of a moving vehicle, Jane. Grace, Grace your mother's mad!................"

"I'm going to my room", I said, without acknowledging anyone.

My head was throbbing, my life was falling apart. It was surreal. I kept thinking that if I pinched myself I'd wake up, but I didn't.

At the first opportunity Grace told me this was reminiscent of her father's behaviour and although I tried to reassure her, this wasn't the case, I had already begun to question my own judgement. I picked up a carrier bag, full of photographs and started looking through them. It was clear in my mind, Andy suffered a mental breakdown. Am I to think Alan is doing the same?

Andy refused to get help fearing he would be labelled 'mad'. He told me one of his aunts had come to England and had been institutionalised here by her husband. He therefore had a deep resentment and fear of the English, describing them as selfish and judgmental, and who could blame him? But, by not dealing with it, Andy took out his frustrations and anger on Grace or me. So is this a pattern, and why am I repeating it!? Why was I having flashbacks? Was Grace right? Did I enjoy being treated badly? So many questions, and no answers. It's amazing how you mind drifts. I shut it out and instead looked through the photographs, showing happier moments. I took off my glasses and closed my eyes for a moment, remembering a happier time in my life.

Maybe if I could get Alan to understand what was going on, then his anger would subside. I knew anger on this level was usually followed by a violent act. I already had bruises on my wrists where Alan had held them so tightly and only let go when I threatened to bite him. I knew from the past, it was better to say little, rather than anger the situation further. So I decided to take a firm stance. I didn't want anyone to get hurt and

felt it better for Alan to come to terms with his anger in his own way.
He came into the room.

"What are you doing, going through old photographs? I am not
your ex-husband!"

Oh shit, I wished he hadn't said that, why would he liken himself to my
ex-husband? I stared harder at the photos, trying to block Alan's
comments out.

"You're all insane, you need therapy, you do, you really do." He
said nodding his head. "How can you slip from one character
into another Jane? I've no respect for Grace because all she
needs is a good kick up the backside and as for you, I wonder
how much you provoked your ex-husband before he hit you.
Because, I tell you what, you've provoked me. You're pathetic.
No wonder men get the blame for everything."

I bit my bottom lip. I didn't need to hear that right now.

"Look Alan, the relationship is deteriorating and it's for the best
we part. This isn't good for any of us."

"I might move out, I'm not sure, but that's my decision not yours
Jane."

"Please, Alan, this isn't good for ANY OF US. I don't want to hurt
you and I don't want things to escalate where anyone gets hurt.
It's like putting a round peg into a square hole, I can't go there
anymore." I could feel my body begin to shake. "It's best for
everyone, think about it Alan."

"I don't want to hear your socialist bullshit. It's your daughter
hovering around all the time. She sneaks around and I can't
move without thinking she's behind me."

I felt for Grace, because all she was doing was making sure that this
time, if, things got out of hand she'd be there to help.

"I can't be bothered with any of you" Alan threw his hands in the
air and started walking up the stairs to bed, talking as he went. He
wouldn't accept anything I had to say, insisting he'd ruined his marriage
because of me.

"It was heaven on earth compared with the hell I'm enduring.
You're mad Jane. You just don't like the truth. I bet your
husband's got a story to tell. I'm going to ring him up and ask his
side of things. It's you Jane, you're responsible and you've
made Grace mad too. You've got a lot to answer for. No wonder
your relationships don't work out. You just don't want to admit it.   I've
talked with friends about you and they all agree. You're mad
both of you." I heard him walk into the bedroom and waited till
he fell asleep.

70

But I stayed awake, his words echoing in my head. This was definitely reminding me of a very unpleasant part of my life, where I had to be vigilant in case Andy attacked me. Why should I feel that way? I know Alan isn't Andy? But why did he keep making comparisons?

With no sleep, anyone can take on monster like proportions, but try as I might, I couldn't reason it out. I spent the rest of those twilight hours sobbing my heart out, having gone through yet another packet of cigarettes; I just couldn't believe what was happening. Was I about to relive the horrors of my past? Please god, no, I'd rather die. I didn't want to be reminded of the past and certainly didn't want to feel the pain but every time Alan and I talked he drew yet another thing from my past. And each one of those insignificant details, he threw back at me in the most horrible way, sending my head into a spin and I revisited the past and the pain I successfully managed to file away.

I woke Grace early the following morning, not that I needed to, she was already awake and suggested we went out.

"Have you seen my glasses Grace?"

"No mum, they were on the chest of drawers last time I saw them." Grace told me Alan scared her and I was beginning to agree.

"Are you sure you haven't seen my glasses?" I said trying to change the subject and then remembered that Alan had been standing next to them the previous day. When we got back I checked behind the chest of drawers and wedged down the back were the glasses.

Alan rang later telling me that he had rung my ex-husband who agreed I was the mad one and suggested I took a good look at myself in the mirror.

"Alan, I need to prevent you from doing something you might regret."

"What nonsense are you coming out with now, Jane? All this socialist bullshit you come out with doesn't make any sense. You're insane, complete straight-jacket job. I feel sorry for your ex-husband. What he had to put up with, it's enough to drive anyone to violence. We've all been there. He just couldn't control it. It's your fault, you brought it upon yourself and what you have done to Grace....you're totally responsible. I would like to come over and talk with both of you, so I'm coming round now."

Why couldn't he understand fault is not a word I wanted to hear and mad is not a label I was prepared to accept? It's just black and white with no grey.

As soon as he arrived he started an onslaught of abuse, covering insane, criminally insane and that he wanted to call the local hospital and have me sectioned.

He told Grace...

"Your mother is mentally sick and the law protects people against that. Don't worry I'll stop her, she is certifiable!"

She looked at him in disbelief but instead of reacting she reverted to the small child, unable to do anything to change what was happening around her. She just sat in the lounge and didn't move. It reminded me of the times when she banged her head on the wall because she couldn't bear to hear me getting hurt when Andy was in one of his rages.

"It was a fact Jane that you were married to someone who was violent and therefore the violence you endured suited you best." He then looked at Grace. "Don't worry, I'll have her locked away."

He turned to me "I'm going to pay your ex-husband a visit and find out who the abuser really was and ask him about the injuries he sustained. I was going to suggest you see a counsellor, Jane but on the other hand don't bother you'd screw their heads in. I've turned down much more attractive and intelligent women than you, and you duped me into this relationship. As I have contributed a lot I'll be sending you an invoice for my time. My normal rate per day is approximately £450. I am appalled at your behaviour. You're filth and should be ashamed of yourself. I wish I'd never met you. You're sick in the head."

"If that's the case Alan, why are you still here!! Oh, and another thing, why did you knock my glasses down behind the chest of drawers, you know I can't move it with my back at the moment?"

"I don't know what you are talking about" he yelled in a manner that sounded decidedly guilty.

"Well it's funny, but I was wearing my spare pair of glasses and put them on the chest of drawers just as you were coming into the room and they disappeared within minutes of me returning and then I forgot all about it but I actually thought you might do something like that then dismissed it, because I didn't think you were that childish. Please just get out, I don't need this."

He ranted something completely incoherent but eventually calmed down. "Look I'm going to make a list of your behavioural problems. It's for your own good" He said trying to compose himself.

Has he gone deaf? I thought, but he continued with the list, which included: irrational behaviour, lying, and only recalling things I wanted to.

"Why don't you respond to some of these allegations Jane?"
"Because they're just your view. I know who I am." I said defiantly.
"Don't get involved with the authorities Jane, you're incapable of being understood. I know you don't like my blunt approach and the truth hurts, doesn't it? "

I looked at him, was I the one ranting and raving? No! So I let him carry on.

I was beginning to hate myself, when I looked in the mirror I no longer liked who I saw. I'd seized the opportunity to get away from the past when I moved but now I was being made to face it all over again. Labelled and made to feel worthless.

He continued with his list.

"You can take this to a psychiatrist. Better still, Jane I'll take it away and type it up properly."

"Ok," I said, agreeing to anything as long as he didn't shout any louder. My head had become sore but worst of all was the pain in my chest, it felt as though my heart was breaking. Here was a man who said he was sensitive and that he would understand but in his face I saw only anger, a man who didn't want to see the damage he was perpetrating on two people who had already been through the grinder.

"Alan, it's best we don't see each other for a while, then we can both address issues, what do you think?"

"You'd like that wouldn't you, but as nothing has been done so far, I'm going to ensure things are sorted for Grace's sake."

"But she's my responsibility not yours." I said angrily.

"Yes and look what you've achieved so far Jane, nothing."

That hurt, in fact that hurt a lot. I'd always worried about what effect the past had really had on Grace. It felt like a knife had gone straight through my heart.

"And you don't get off the hook that easily, Jane .... Look, Jane, I'm beyond approach, having only had one long-term relationship which lasted 25 years......... I know you wouldn't understand that. The behaviour of both you and your daughter is nothing less than a couple of 'oiks'. You really deserved what happened to you."

I took another drag on a cigarette and wondered why me.

"Jane, I've a much longer list of the nice things about you. This is your only chance to make a relationship work. You've got to try harder."

I found myself looking at the wall just as I'd done all those years ago, studying the cracks, trying to focus on something else and not listen to the comments which were being thrown in my direction.

I tried to talk, but Alan wasn't listening and didn't want to leave. Day turned to night and that evening I slept in the spare room. In the early hours Alan got dressed, saying he was going out. He came back an hour later and walked into the spare room to ask what I was doing,

"Please, I don't want another argument Alan."

"I feel the same way, so that's enough for today OK?" He was making me feel like some kind of 'guinea pig' and part of some kind of experiment.

He tried to talk with me later that day and now it was Grace who was causing him a problem.

"Jane, she's virtually a basket case and you're nothing better than a 'slapper' from South London. I've got to go out now, I'll see you later."

It felt I'd been crying for days. I was so tired and I didn't want to hear anymore. Who did he think he was and why on earth won't he just leave? I knew from the past that there was no help available. What I didn't understand was why he kept coming back? When he did return I asked him to sit down.

"Look, let's just split up. This isn't doing anyone any good, please, just stop it now. I don't understand what's going on here but I can't take anymore." I looked in his eyes hoping for a glimmer of light that told me he understood what I was saying but it just made him angrier. After calming down he told me, he just felt insecure. "But why, I havn't done anything to make you feel that way Alan?"

"Lets go out and get some fresh air Jane."

I explained to Grace we were trying to sort things out and that it was better we discussed things away from the house.

We both agreed this was destroying each other and that horrible things had been said. He said he felt he was on the verge of a nervous breakdown and just when I thought he was beginning to understand himself, he went in to overdrive...........................

"You're filth, I wished I'd never met you or your bloody daughter. I'm not at all surprised Andy hit you. You are driving me insane, just like you did with your husband. You should be made accountable for what you do."

I sat down on the ground, he had the ability to draw me in close by seeming sincere and then slash me to pieces. I waited whilst he finished his verbal onslaught and we returned home, only Alan's views mattered, if at any point I tried to interject he would dismiss my comments as bullshit. Accusing me of living in a fantasy world.

Grace didn't want to be party to any of what was going on and I suggested she went away for a few days. Driving her to London the following day to stay with friends.
Alan wanted Grace and I to see a psychologist, and I agreed. I knew she wasn't coping at all well and was worried about the damaging affect this was having on her. He had arranged for he and I to met a friend of his in London who worked with young people and it seemed to go well.
However, Alan continued accusing both Grace and her friends of playing mind games with him, saying she was trying to get into his head but wouldn't succeed and trying to convince him otherwise was futile.
I decided getting outside help was an excellent idea, however, trying to convince Grace to agree was another matter entirely.

"How on earth can he blame me for his own problems! I just want to stay out of it mum. Does he really think this is normal? What about his kids, they've already mentioned to me that it's him?"
"I know it's difficult but and we can't bring his kids into it, and it might be a good idea to see someone who may be able to help."
Grace had developed blisters on her body, she was clearly suffering from stress.

"Look Grace I'm worried about you sweetheart, we need to bring this out into the open somehow and maybe this is a way of doing it. I can't very well phone the police, they won't believe us, not with our past. And you heard Alan say the Police wanted to know if there was any mental instability in our family. You can't prove psychological abuse, it's his word against ours and he's got friends here, this isn't our 'neck of the woods', remember. We are on his patch, so who do you think people are going to believe? You just have to trust me, please."

When I returned Alan repeated telling me Grace and her friends were playing mind games with him and that he wouldn't stand for it.
"Do you remember when she was talking about having a family of her own and how she would like to bring the grandchildren round. I doubt any man would be interested in her." He said.
"That's cruel Alan!"

"Ah, just face facts, Jane. Who'd be interested in her. If there were a spectrum, she would go out with a man at the lower end, face it. Where does she get her money from?"

"She worked in London and has her own monies. She's only 19 and just needs to get a job here." I said, trying to defend a position I really didn't need to defend and being hurt by his comments.

I was beginning to get the shakes again, I knew I had allowed Alan to get too close. I should never have told him about my life because now he was going to destroy us with it. He had nothing but contempt for both of us.

"OK, you just don't want to listen. I'm just going to go; I don't need this grief. I'm going to sort the flat out. I need to keep busy. I'll speak with you later Jane."

The flat? That means he kept it on, so why doesn't he just go and live there and leave us alone?

He rang later

"Is Grace going to get better? She reverted to a 6-year-old the other day. She's getting between us and seems quite happy to destroy my life. I don't want that but I'm here to help. I'm going to use the flat as a 'bolt-hole' for when things get bad."

It was at times like these I was completely lost for words. I wondered how he would like it should I talk of his children in that way, but said nothing, after all it meant he was distancing himself from us and that meant Grace and I could start to put the foundations back into our life. Inside I just wanted to go back to London, where you are treated as an individual but I couldn't tell Grace because she had the courage to move here, away from everyone she knew and now she was being treated as little more that excess baggage.

So Alan stayed out of our lives for a while and somehow I got the impression he had a close female friend other than his PA who was advising him. We'd meet up for lunch but there was always another flash point and I was beginning to feel caught in a familiar situation.

The phone rang

"Hi Jane, how are things? You know Grace is going to take another 20 years to sort out. I'm too old for all that. I want to get on with my life. She's running up your bills and should be left in rags. But you're not strong enough to deal with it. She's controlling our lives and I'm embarrassed when friends ask about her. I don't want her anywhere near my children.

But I could write a paper on this. You are a real case"

"That's ridiculous. What do you expect me to do and what do you mean by case? All the arguments haven't helped, she's suffering from depression and who can blame her."

"The arguments are as a result of Grace, CAN'T YOU SEE THAT JANE!!"

Try as I might, he wouldn't be dissuaded.

Grace has gone back into herself, not wanting to do anything but sit in her room. As for me, I just felt sick and ill with everything that had happened around us. It seemed we were in the middle of nowhere and with no friends and family around us and thoughts of suicide were creeping into my mind.

Later that evening Alan came over, saying he needed to pick up a few things.

"Jane, it's you who's the abuser. You've already messed up other people's lives and that includes Grace but I'll stop you by informing the authorities."

"Fine, just get it over with. Ring who you like." I said and went upstairs, after telling him I needed to go out for a while.

I popped my head around the door of Grace's room

"I need to get some fresh air, I can't listen to Alan's accusations anymore. He's here collecting more of his things."

I collected my keys, jumped into the car and went for a drive.

Grace was so worried she got my brother George to call on the mobile.

"Jane, I don't know what's going on but Grace just rang me and she's worried about you."

I laughed."You don't think I am a bad person, do you George?"

"Don't be daft, its not you, its just Alan trying to get into your head. Don't let him!"

"But why. What makes someone do that?"

"Maybe, he just enjoys it, Jane. Be strong, go home and tell Alan to leave."

"How can anyone enjoy hurting someone. Look I've tried but he seems to think he's on a mission to rescue Grace from me or vice versa whichever the day of the week it is and he just won't listen"

"Just do it Jane! Go home now."

Having struggled for years to get out of an abusive relationship, the thought of confronting someone else was quite a daunting task.

I couldn't face the prospect of a confrontation when I didn't know the ending!

Nevertheless, I carried out my brother's wishes, returning home, where Alan was waiting.

> "You've got it all wrong Jane. It's not me that should leave but Grace. I've worked it all out and feel sorry for the men in your life. I've had years of mental abuse from my wife but you've been the worst abuser of all. If there were another party present to witness this, then I would be able to sue you out of existence. You're mad Jane"

How familiar, I thought, a little while ago he wanted to sue Grace for defamation of character when she became worried about me and had stayed with a friend in London. He had taken her text messages to me asking if things were OK, as rude and started ranting about making her penniless when we were married. I had completely forgotten about the fact that, we actually got engaged, which I remember being a wonderfully romantic day, but within two weeks he'd asked for the ring back! It was as it he couldn't stand the fact we could be happy, so he would make a blissfully wonderful moment turn into something awful so you remember it for the pain or file it away and not remember it at all. He wasn't completely without emotion and would always feel guilty afterwards, arranging a little holiday or trip somewhere by way of compensation and that was how it began to feel. But the trips, designed to make things better, were also dependant on what mood Alan was in, so the ring had become a symbol of something else he could emotionally batter me with, and eventually I just couldn't cope with it anymore and gave it back to him for good.

> "Look, Jane I'll move out tomorrow it's too late for me to go back to the flat tonight and I'm worried about you. I'm worried about what Grace will do to you. I keep going back to the flat becauseI can't take anymore abuse having suffered it for years."

He repeated this over and over again as if he needed to reassure himself of its significance.

> "Alan, why would you want to be with someone you thought about in that way?"

He ignored me.

> "I'm going to make a tea and then I'm going to bed." He went

upstairs, leaving me standing in the kitchen completely aghast, thinking, why on earth doesn't he just leave?!!! And as I followed later, I wondered how he could sleep in the same room. The master bedroom had an ensuite, so I took a bath, made sure he was asleep before creeping out to the spare room. I lay there thinking; he doesn't seem to like it here, this is now my home and yet he feels he can do what he wants and talk to Grace and me anyway he feels fit. How does he rationalise this view???????!

Next morning he was up early collecting more things from the bedroom and taking them to his car. I waited for a while and then got dressed. He told me the car was almost full so was unable to take more and asked if he could return later. I didn't have a problem with that and told him so and before long he was back.

I tried my hardest to stay out of his way but he was intent on having the last word, muttering inaudible comments as he went. And then he asked for the sheets he'd brought over with him, plus duvet and pillows. As he had slept on them the night before, I simply pointed him in the direction of the bedroom.

"It's Ok, Jane I'll just strip it." He marched off and I followed, currious to see that he would go to such lengths and watched, as he took off the sheets, folding them neatly and making comment on any mark he found on the mattress, insinuating they were from other men.

Rage is a funny thing, because it was at this point I lost my cool, as this was the man I had given my love to. I Screamed at him that he was not the kind of person to such a judgement and was probably just mirroring his own behaviour. I had bottled up so much it needed to all come out and it did all at once, complete verbal overload, including the inevitable swear words that slipped into my vocabulary. I really can't recall exactly what I said. Needless to say, I'm sure it wasn't pleasant.

I had tried to keep quiet, but he just kept going on and on. I knew only too well not to confront a situation in this way but it was difficult.

I'm sure it's easier if you don't care for someone, because you can deal with it in a cold and clinical way but when you are emotionally bonded, it hurts like hell and hell is exactly where I felt I had been.

"No wonder you don't have any friends Jane they all know who you are and if they don't I'm going to ring them and tell them. They should be protected from someone like you."

"Oh, go ahead Alan. My friends know me well enough not to listen to you and I don't want to hear anymore defamatory remarks about my character."

"Well you're certainly not a lady, using language like that."

"No probably not in your books but who cares about your point of view. You're not exactly a gentleman."

Alan had wounded me so deeply, that I literally physically start to shake when he erupts, and that hasn't happened to me in years. The deepest hurt was he betrayed my trust. So was any of it worth it? Have I learnt anything from this relationship? Well the answer is that I probably won't let anyone get that close again.

He went off, returning a short while later to reaffirm his view that I was an abuser and that he would be telling the counsellor and the authorities and asked for clothing he had bought me because he felt he could find another woman whom they would fit.

He eventually went, can't remember his final words, helped by me throwing some of the clothes on top of the bonnet of his car. Around 4pm he sent a text message "Jane, what we're doing is so very wrong! I love u and we must talk and not throw this away - it's just too precious." And an hour later he was back again to tell me he didn't want to leave without being friends

> "You should have thought about that a while ago."
> "You hate me don't you Jane?"

I didn't reply.

> He left again, calling me from his mobile, "I don't want us to become enemies."
> "We already are Alan." The phone went dead.

I remember a phrase he used regarding his ex-wife, how she was now outside the circle and fair game and how his daughter told me her mother was scared of him. Personally, I feel sick, have a pain in my chest and my brain feels it's been turned to mush.

Later he popped a card through the letterbox, which read **'my dear Jane, I wanted to say so much to you today but you would not listen. The important thing is my profound thanks for what has been the best year in my life. My memories are overwhelmingly good - some of the happiest times ever, for me have been spent with you. You are a wonderful person but you do have a foul temper, which I find impossible to live with. Please don't think, I think too badly of Grace. It's an extremely touchy subject with you and it has become impossible to discuss, giving rise to the sort of outburst you demonstrated again this weekend. She will get sorted, so just chill out -its tough for everyone. One thing you have to know - I do love you more than I can put into words. I'll get over you but I'll never forget you!'**

80

Phew, well at last I can start getting my life back in order.

But it didn't end there, a couple of days later, he rang to say he wanted to come along to see the counsellor with me because he felt I needed the support.

"Meet me at the flat, please Jane."

I went along happy to be friends, if he only realised he had a problem. When I arrived he was smoking cannabis, which he used as a crutch to help him get through life, I know because I have been there. He told me, he still needed to gain access to the house, he had a telephone line put in and it would take some weeks to get a new at the flat. He suggested we act reasonably toward one another, because it wasn't his fault, I had a daughter who was screwed up by her past. I ignored the comment.

"Look I don't have any objection as long as you let me know." I said thinking that he needed counselling.

"I want to try and support you on this Jane, no one has been there in the past and I really want to help. Grace is a big problem and I need to protect people from her?!"

"What on earth are you talking about, don't you understand anything!?"

"It's likely Grace is not recoverable. She needs support and a father figure, you can't do it on your own."

"Alan, I have spoken with her and since we moved here she's found things difficult and has been worried about the arguments."

"I know I can be hot-headed, Jane but that's normal in relationships everyone argues, it's just that you're not used to normality. Anyway she was like that before, I met you. You told me she went through a depression."

"Look, that happens to lots of kids at some stage in their life, she got let down by the school and people around her that's all, and I'm not prepared to give up on my daughter. It's only a matter of time till she gets employment here."

"Then let me help, please. We do have something special. I don't want to throw it away. I told you we can help each other."

I said I would think about it and went back home "Grace let's give it a go and maybe we can dispel some of the myths associated with the past, it would help bring us together as a family."

We agreed he could come along to the counselling sessions and afterwards he spoke with Grace.

"I know you're worried, I'm going to take your mum's money

but that's not the case. I've plenty of my own and my money is your mum's money."

Grace was clearly confused. "My mum is clever enough to look after herself", she replied, sharply.

"But do you know what I do?" Alan replied.

"No." Grace said, beginning to relax a little.

"Well, I put together deals, that generate money, I'm receiving a cheque soon for a large sum. I made a million when I was not, much older than you. I know having lots of money is not a life you're used to." He said, looking into her eyes and trying to reach an understanding

"My Mum and Dad ran a business and there were times when we were wealthy and times when we were poor." Retorted Grace.

Irritated by her response, he changed the subject, suggesting instead we went for something to eat and afterwards dropped us home.

Grace was furious. "Why are you taking me to see someone when you know he's the one with the problem?"

"Please don't be angry with me, I am beginning to realise that if we don't do something about it then, even though we've moved away from your Dad this stigma is going to follow us wherever we go. I know it's hard but maybe he wants everything to work out and don't forget the counsellors, aren't stupid they're trained to see problems. At least he's trying and he wants to be there and there's nowhere else to turn, no one else has ever tried to understand." I said trying to sound reassuring.

"No he doesn't Mum he's quite happy for us to be labelled as mad just to clear his own conscience. Why can't you see that. I'm beginning to think you're mad and you enjoy being abused. He's called you all those names. Don't you see what he's doing, he's undermining your confidence and I'm losing respect for you."

"Please don't, it hurts enough already Grace. It's a bit late if you are worried about labels, we've moved into his patch remember, no-one knows us here. People judge because we live in a blame society. It's up to us to break down those barriers and show people we're bigger than the problem, don't you see?"

"Why do you do it? Why do you try so hard? It won't work. I've heard some of things he has said to you."

"Look Grace, you do have some issues about the past and you do need to address them at some point. But by running away or closing ourselves off from people only allows them to view us in certain way. He might be able to help. It was his contacts that found us a counsellor. Maybe he is sincere, and just doesn't know how to handle things. You know I've always wanted a normal home and haven't been able to offer you that."

"Wake-up Mum, I know what you want, but he's not interested. He's just using you because it's convenient. He doesn't have anywhere to go. You're falling into a trap. He doesn't care about you, otherwise he wouldn't have said the things he's said. The walls in this place are so thin, I've heard some of the things. It's like he took a 'sledge hammer' to your head and he's trying to do the same to mine. I couldn't do anything about the past but I will if he tries to hurt you, I am older enough now."

I smiled and suddenly felt quite proud of her, and a tear formed in my eye when I remembered how she had tried to protect me when she was tiny.

"Thanks, Grace, but maybe the counselling will help me understand myself and if Alan wants to go through it too, it will help all of us in the long term."

"I know it won't work Mum, people don't change."

"Then do it for me, please Grace. The counsellor told me 20% of men do change. He's probably got something in his own past he needs to face. We've all got demons. I promise you don't have to come along again, if you don't want to."

"Alright, but I'm not mad. I wish we'd never moved here, I hate it here. I did it because you told me things would be better and look what happened. He doesn't even want me to talk to his kids!"

"I know Grace", I said biting my bottom lip and fighting back the tears "but I promise, I won't let anyone hurt you. Trust me. Surely the counsellor can't be that blind. I've got to have faith that someone will understand. The police can't do anything."

Things improved Alan has given us the space we need and as we don't see him as much, so I decided to look around for part-time work and Grace has registered with the local job agencies.

But really it was just a lull before the storm as I nonchantly picked up the phone one day.

"Grace is destroying my business. I've had to take an office in town for £5,000 a year."

"What? Grace isn't like that." But a row ensued and he slammed the phone down on me.

Grace just looked at me...

"I told you it wouldn't work. He's only interested in how much money he is losing." She whispered.

Later he rang again to tell me he'd managed to do a deal with a company and would share their facilities in return for work, suggesting I did the same and put all my office stuff there.

"Thanks for the offer but as I no longer run a business, there would be little point in shifting my paperwork around the countryside. I'm starting a job on Monday for three weeks because I need to focus and keep my feet on the ground Alan."

"That's a good idea, Jane. What are you doing?"

"I'm going to be working with children in the local community centre."

"Well, good luck."

The job was quite a challenge but I thoroughly enjoyed it because it got me out of the house and back meeting people again.

Alan was popping over once a day to collect e-mails, normally early evening when I returned from work. He told me he was going to be wealthy and that I'd helped during the divorce. He went for a clean break and as both parties had agreed it had been quite quick in its deliverance.

"I'm sorry about some of the things that happened, Jane. I have been under a lot of pressure including the Inland Revenue and have had to pay a lot in taxes, so things were a bit fraught."

"That's OK, we are none of us very good under pressure." I said.

By coincidence it had worked to his advantage because new deals were being offered to him.

"I was happy to help as long as you can do me a favour and address some of those anger issues you've got"

He smiled, "Well, you have been a great help. Look I've got to go now, catch you later."

Grace had been listening to the conversation.

"Don't you think that's strange Mum? He's always talking about money, and yet he gets upset when you try and cancel things that he arranges last minute, just because he needs to get away. Why should it worry him if he's got all this money?"

"I don't know Grace, he probably needs to get away from the problems with his family. Divorce is very stressful, he's given all his assets to his wife. It's difficult for anyone to start all over again let alone at the age of 50. You know how stressed out I've been over the move. I thought I was on the verge of a nervous breakdown and I'm still having trouble with my back, after all this time."

"Maybe." Grace said looking at the floor.

"Grace, will you just stop thinking for a while, come on I'll buy you lunch."

Later that evening Alan's brother, Peter, rang. It was obvious he was aware of our situation and asked if Alan was at the flat.

"Yes, I think so, you should be able to catch him on the mobile."

"Is it true your ex-husband used to hit you?" Peter asked.

"Yeah, Yes, he did. Did Alan tell you?"

"I'm sorry to hear that Jane."

"It's OK it was years ago, these things happen."

"You know Alan's got a bit of a temper don't you?"

"Yes, I've been on the receiving end of it, what's it all about Peter?"

"Oh, he just takes things out on those around him, when he's under stress. Don't take it personally. If you want someone to talk to, I can be a sounding block, if you like."

"Thanks, I'll keep that in mind. Well as I said he's on the mobile, see you soon."

I put the phone down and then felt the need to ring the counsellor,

"I'm not sure about all this, it's becoming painful." I told her.

"It could get worse. It's not you Jane. Alan just doesn't realise what he's doing but I'm here to help. He's emotionally stuck."

"What does that mean?" I enquired.

"Well, he needs to get in contact with his emotions."

"Oh great, now I'm caught up in something that I just know is going to cause me more pain."

"Do you want to continue Jane?"

"Can it be stopped?" I said pleadingly.

"Well, as I said 20% of men do seek help and are cured but it's up to him. He's got to take ownership of the problem."

"Ok, let's go ahead", I said, "I need to carry on for all of us, otherwise Grace will think this is the way life is."

I lit another cigarette, it was becoming a habit, my nerves were in shreds and I needed something to calm me down. I didn't feel there was any point in talking with his brother, as it might make matters worse, I also heard he had a temper himself, so I didn't favour the idea of getting in between them.

I saw Alan later that evening and we talked over the problems, he was smoking quite a bit of cannabis and now exhibiting signs of paranoia.

> "Alan the way you speak to me at times reminds me of my past. I can't deny that. And the things you say to me send me back there and I start shaking."
>
> "But I'm not your ex-husband" He said indignantly.
>
> "I know that, but something is happening and you can't keep doing this for the rest of your life."
>
> "Maybe its that bloody book, you've been writing"
>
> "No, it's not that, Alan. I'm reacting to a real situation here. Maybe you should look into your past, instead of analysing and attacking mine."
>
> "Look my brother had some issues but I'm fine. How dare you talk about my past when you are incapable of having a relationship with anyone Jane."

I sighed and didn't pursue it, instead talked of complete trivia, then left. He rang a couple of hours later in tears.

> "I'm finding this all too difficult and I need to talk to you."
>
> "But Alan, its late."
>
> "Please Jane, I don't want to be on my own."
>
> "OK, I'll be there in half an hour."

We decided, delving into the past too much wasn't good for either of us,so for the next few weeks everything, although a little strained, improved.

Christmas came and went, although my family couldn't cope with the situation they found it all too difficult and I didn't blame them. As far as they were concerned, I was back where I started.

To help Grace become mobile I bought her a car as an incentive to pass her test. Then booked up some more lessons. I needed to give her some independence. She'd already had a few lessons in London, so it was just a matter of preparing her for her test. A neighbour recommended an excellent instructor who Grace quite liked and Alan offered to help by going out with her occasionally, as he now believes she just lacks in confidence.

However as New Year passed, Alan regressed.

> "I'm going to write a list of the things I can't accept. You both threw me out of this house and I will never forget it. I will never put myself in a situation where a woman does that to me again. My wife would never do such a thing."

I agreed, trying to pacify what I knew to be another row looming.

But he kept going.

"I don't care what led up to being thrown out, the facts are as they are. You've knocked my confidence. You just want someone you can keep under the thumb." With that he upt and left.

He had the capacity to make me really happy and then really miserable. It was like months of sublime happiness, followed by a hole in the head. I had never been that close to anyone.

I found it hard to see his point of view at times and he refused to accept mine, choosing instead to bring up the past by way of defence.

He rang a bit later and asked me to come over and talk. I said I would but couldn't stay long.

"You're a very jealous person and just want to control me. You've behaved just like your ex-husband and are controlling your daughter's life. She will hate men, if she doesn't already but I'll rescue her from you!!"

"What?" I stood in complete amazement. The heated way in which he said this made me angry but I bit my tongue.

"You just can't face it can you, you're the abuser. Even the counsellor agrees with me. You don't know what a real relationship's like. You're a cold fish and can't have real emotions but you should consider the fact that you're damaged not by your ex-husband but by your father."

"Who?" I said looking confused.

"And I think right now I need to call a doctor and have you sedated Jane."

I walked towards the door

"Who the hell do you think you are? I don't need to listen to this crap,"

But he snatched my car keys, demanding I came back inside.

"I'm not going to let you drive in that state Jane."

"What state?"

"Come and sit down. Look at this." He produced a photo of a woman shaking her fists. "Look closely". I looked at the photo. "That's my face!"

"It's you, you don't remember do you? You're mad and you've ruined your daughter's life. You've also ruined the lives of your past partners too, I was happy in my life until I met you. I've been speaking with the counsellor and she agrees with me. You don't think for a minute I would have let you go along to see someone without some feed back do you? She's been e-mailing me, look here's her e-mail address. There are some very important people living around here and as I've lived here most of my life, I'm not without contacts."

"Alan, I need to get out of here, I can't listen to this"

"Oh, you can go alright Jane but first give me back the shoes and gloves I bought you."

"You can have the gloves but I need the shoes right now."

I threw the gloves on the floor.

The thought that I'd been diagnosed as an abuser and had ruined my daughter's life was too much to bear.

"I won't drive home, I'll walk." I said, thinking how the hell could the counsellor get it so wrong and where did the photo come from, I don't remember it!

"If you do Jane. I'll phone the police."

"Then be my guest, maybe they can give me a lift." I ignored him and walked out of the door, deep in thought.

I walked along the pathway that led from the estate to the main road. I didn't want to listen to anymore. I was deeply hurt, upset and completely confused. Surely the counsellor had worked it out, but thinking about it, she'd told me I had an anger issue............me?!!!!

Well, if I didn't when I started, I certainly do now.

It was a cold night and the air was crisp but somewhat sobering. Being away from him made me feel better as I the trod the unlit path toward the main road. What I didn't recognise was the gradual breakdown I was suffering.

Alan drove past and stopped. The temperature outside was freezing

"You won't make it back on foot. Get in." I was feeling sick and had a terrible headache.

"Don't be a fool, get in. You don't even know your way round these parts."

He was right, even if I got to the main road, there were no pavements or street lights to light my way, so I got in, whereupon he continued telling me I was mad.

We got back to the flat. I was cold and shaking uncontrollably.

"Here have some of this" and he passed me a joint.

"Look I've lived in this area most of my life, I'm well known here and all I'm trying to do is help you Jane but first you have to admit it's you. There are a lot of dignitaries living here, and government officials. It's a known fact women have been abusing men for years. I've taken advice on the matter. I've built homes for people in this area, people are reliant on me for their future. My children are reliant on me, I can't have my integrity attacked in this way by the likes of you. I'm going to have to do something about you, you know that don't you?"

"Like what? If I'm mad I'll consider what I do with my future and that of my daughter."

"You've used the word mad too often, Jane and anyway, it won't be you that will do something about this, it will be me. Now I'm going to count the amount of times you mention the word mad"

He was good at this jumping the conversation round and round till you began to think that you had labelled yourself.

He took his diary and started writing things down. Setting down 'the paper chain' as he called it and then started taking pictures, telling me he was keeping a record of changes in my behaviour.

"I can write a paper on you."

"Alan, shut the fuck up, I can't take much more of this. You're sick."

"No one will believe you Jane."

"GIVE ME MY KEYS." I screamed and searched the flat but he'd hidden them.

"Sit down, you're not going anywhere. Who taught you that filthy language? I bet I can guess"

He continued talking trying to get me to agree with his analysis of the situation, telling me that he had a lot of influence and it was about time women were shown as the abusers they really were.

"You can't do that!! Alan, you'll destroy both of us. Look just let me go and Grace and I will move away we don't need anymore trouble." But he went on.

His flat was on a private estate, on an unmade road and although I tried he continued to block any attempt on my part to escape. As time went by, I found myself agreeing to anything he said.

"If you're correct" I said, feeling the tears rolling down my face and for the first time in my life questioning what I had done to my daughter.

"And this was something I don't recognise in myself then I've got nothing left. I really couldn't live with the thought that I was the abuser and had hurt people, including my daughter."

"Why did you consider walking home?" He interceded

"What?" I said vaguely "Oh, I just don't like feeling trapped."

"Look we're all here to help, here smoke some of this, it will make you feel better and help you sleep"

By now it was 3.00 am and any further thoughts of leaving were futile, I was exhausted.

Eventually I fell asleep and the following morning Alan woke first

"What we've done was so destructive Jane. I've had 25 years

with a woman who was an inveterate liar and I don't want it anymore. I've had enough of women. Whenever I try to help I just get kicked in the teeth. I feel unwelcome at your home due to Grace and she's controlling our lives and you've made her what she is, you're just too close to see. If you think she got through all that unscathed, you'd better wake up. What we need to know is how badly damaged she is."

"I'm sorry I don't accept Grace has a problem just some issues that's all and what you've done this evening is unforgivable." I said, "how could you?"

He handed me my car keys

"Look we can work this out between us, it's time you got the support you need Jane and I'm here to help. You'd best get back, Grace will be woried about you."

"Don't worry, I'm going."

I left feeling battered and bruised, not physically just mentally. I kept telling myself that I should be stronger. I decided not to mention too much to Grace, she would only worry, and got ready for work as usual. My own confidence had taken quite a pounding and I was grateful to have something else to concentrate on for a while and working with children was a real joy.

On the way, Alan rang my mobile

"I want my things, I can't get access to your house"

"But you've got a key!" I said increduously

"You and your daughter are causing my business to fail. I've already spent £165,000 on you."

"That's ridiculous Alan, and if it's true, then I can't afford to go out with you anymore. Look I can't talk now, I've just arrived for work. I'll speak with you later ."

"You're always cancelling things and putting the phone down on me Jane", but I didn't listen.

Work allowed me to cut off and become completely focused. It must have been about 5.30 pm when I got home. We'd arranged to go out that evening with Alan and his children and a text came through on my mobile asking if I was still going. Instead of replying, I went to my room and lay on the bed, it was all too much for me. One minute he didn't want Grace to have anything to do with his children, then he did, one minute I'm mad then I'm not, Grace is a problem then she's not. This guy is a real mind fuck. The photograph worried me, it was my face but my body...........no.

Grace had gone to the trouble of cooking a meal and was anxious to know what was happening.

90

"Please leave me alone, I can't think right now." I said and she went away whereupon I drifted into a deep sleep.

I woke to find Grace standing by the bed. It felt like I'd been asleep for only a few minutes, although Grace insisted it was at least half an hour.

"Alan's kids are here, what do you want me to do Mum?"

"Just let them in, I'll be down in a short while."

Alan's daughter came to my room and popped her head round the door.

"Are you OK, Jane. You look dreadful? Dad is always like this when things go wrong in business but it's soon forgotten."

"But this isn't the first time Alan's done this."

"I know", she said, "he did it to mum. She didn't even like being in the same room with him at times. It stems from his father."

I confided in her that he was going for counselling, which was positive.

"Then he must think a lot of you because he wouldn't go for mum. Do you think counselling will help?"

"Well, I guess first of all he's got to recognise he has a problem, if you support me, I'll try." I said trying not to sound too concerned.

"We'll do our best, are you going to come to the cinema? Dad is going to be here soon"

"I don't know what to do, I really don't feel that well."

Alan had two children Peter and Samantha and both were aware of his behaviour. Sam was more understanding, as she knew the history of the family.

"Mum, Alan's here!!"

Grace sounded perplexed, not knowing what to do for the best, so I went to open the door, welcomed him in and sat down to eat the dinner Grace had prepared. No-one said anything and afterwards we went to the cinema. I couldn't help feeling the awkwardness from all parties but the evening was fine and later after his kids had gone home, I raised the subject of taking in his post.

"Look Alan, as you're not here very much, I feel unhappy about receiving your business correspondence. You said you were going to take care of it, last time we spoke but nothing's happened."

"Do you really think so little of me Jane, that you think I'd do something to your property?"

"I'm sure you wouldn't but the way things have been going lately, I don't know where I stand Alan, so can you just deal with it."

"OK, Jane, I wanted to include you in my business plans but I won't now. I'll redirect the post. Does that make you happy?"

"Yes, thank you." No more was said on the matter but it clearly upset him.

I went off to work as normal, the following day. Alan stayed over saying he had an appointment locally and would be back around midday to collect his post from Grace. However, when I got home around 5.45pm, Grace told me she hadn't heard from him. At 6.30 pm he rang,

"I don't feel welcome at the house. The problem with Grace is bigger than I imagined." He stated.

"I don't understand"

"Jane, it's you who's is the abuser."

"Oh, really, not that again, please Alan."

Never once did he question what he said. He just carried on goading, analysing and criticising.

"I can't understand the change. Have you been speaking with someone?" I asked.

And then he mentioned the counsellor's name.

"Have you been in touch?" I enquired.

"No, I just know what's going on and I'm not prepared to waste my life. You'll never be able to have a relationship with anyone; that's my guess. I just want to come over and collect some more of my things."

He eventually did just that and went on about how he'd been treated by us. Grace sat in the lounge as he continued talking about her and telling me I was an abuser.

"Look I don't understand you at all but if you feel this way then we should part even as friends and I respect your wishes."

"That's not the right answer Jane! You act just like your ex-husband and Grace is a control freak, controlling my life. She's going to be with you for the next 45 years but I don't have   t o put up with it!"

"OK. No that's right Alan, you don't have to put up with anything you don't want to."

I knew Grace was already upset but he didn't moderate his tone and kept repeating

"She'll ruin your life Jane, why don't you wake up!"

He kept comparing her with other children, he knew.

"Why don't you come to the flat with me to get away from her, if not I'm going to have to say goodbye."

I looked at him and watched as he turned and left.

Then spent another night without sleep, mulling things over in my head.

The following day, I got back from work around 6.15, and was surprised to find Grace's car missing!! I knew how upset she'd been the night before and thought it odd. I called her mobile but it went straight through to her ansaphone, I just knew she must be with Alan.

Alan returned with Grace around 7.30 pm, I was so relieved to see her.

"I told you Jane, I just want to help that's all. I can give Grace the confidence she needs. I'll help get her through her test"

I didn't say anything, in fact I didn't know what to say but as dinner was already prepared I asked if he wanted to stay for something to eat.

This went on for days with Alan coming and going.

"Jane we shouldn't be doing this to each other. We're both feeling the affects of the counsellor. Why don't we take a trip and talk things over."

"I don't know Alan, I don't really need this. I might move back to London."

"But that might be a mistake for Grace."

"Grace will decide what she wants to do. At the moment she wants to go back too and I want the best for her."

"Do you know what is best for Grace? Please let's go away and talk about it. Look I love you and I know you love me. I gave you my ring remember and asked you to marry me?"

I had completely forgotten about that, it seemed a million miles and too far from reality because no sooner had it been on my finger, Alan was asking for it back.

"Look at me Jane, look into my eyes, I mean it, you and Grace just need some understanding. I love you and I'll give you all the support you need. I'm not going to give up, I'm not like the other men in your life. I mean everything, I say, you can trust me. I know you've never had that before but now you have someone who has your best interests at heart."

He never gave in till he had the answer he wanted. He was always so persuasive, so charming and so believable, that I found myself agreeing to go away for a few days to talk things over. Where he was again his charming self and on our return, I felt he really was making progress and wanted to make things work, not just for Grace but for his kids too.

Our return coincided with a meeting at the counsellors. After which, yet another argument took place.

> "I wish I had a tape recorder to prove to people what you're really like."

He yelled and left, retreating to his flat. I reached a point some time ago of not arguing back, instead I told him he should be with someone he actually liked. Maybe it was a 'learnt hurt' from his past, but until he addressed it there was little anyone could do to help. At one point, when he came over, he'd taken to sharpening a large carving knife that I kept in the kitchen, insisting they needed to be kept sharp. He thought the knife was one used by my ex-husband to frighten me all those years ago. However, it was more the noise as he sharpened it that really set my teeth on edge. But Grace also noticed the habit, as if he wanted to know whether we would remember.

The counsellor had told me I was suffering from Post Traumatic Stress Syndrome? Which I didn't really understand. All I knew was there are times where I can't stop shaking and have been smoking myself to death which is a direct result of the relationship with Alan. At the counsellors, Alan only wants to concentrate on my past which is making me ill.

I tried to get myself registered with a doctor locally but was having trouble, so Alan took me to an emergency doctor to discuss my back, which was still plaguing me, only to be informed I was out of the area.

Strangely enough, I later found out that Alan's doctor's was only a few miles from our home but he hadn't suggested we could be added to the register.

A Poison Tree

I was angry with my friend:
I told my wrath, my wrath did end.
I was angry with my foe:
I told it not, my wrath did grow.

And I watered it in fears,
Night and morning with my tears;
And I sunned it with smiles,
And with soft deceitful wiles.

And it grew both day and night,
Till it bore an apple bright;
And my foe beheld it shine,
And he knew that it was mine,

And into my garden stole
When the night had veiled the pole:
In the morning glad I see
My foe outstretched beneath the tree.

William Blake

The Tiger

Tiger! Tiger! burning bright
In the forests of the night,
What immortal hand or eye
Could frame thy fearful symmetry

In what distant deeps or skies
Burnt the fire of thine eyes?
On what wings dare he aspire?
What the hand dare seize the fire?

And what shoulder, and what art,
Could twist the sinews of thy heart?
And when they heart began to beat,
What dread hand, and what dread feet?

What the hammer? what the chain?
In what furnace was thy brain?
What the anvil? what dread grasp
Dare its deadly terrors clasp?

When the stars threw down their spears,
And watered heaven with their tears,
Did he smile his work to see?
Did he who made the lamb make thee?

Tiger! Tiger burning bright
In the forests of the night,
What immortal hand or eye,
Dare frame they fearful symmetry

William Blake

Chapter 5

The relationship with Alan

Alan's done another disappearing act, I haven't spoken with him for days but I do feel better in myself. The countryside is still beautiful and I take solace in the thought that although I'm left with no answers, I'm beginning to recognise a pattern.

I have started to read a book recommended to me by the counsellor. It states, 'people who devalue their partner do it in such a way as to make them feel powerless and chronically insecure'. That is exactly how I felt. I've been made to feel that I've achieved nothing in my life and am a worthless individual.

But that's not really me and I'm worth more than that, so why am I involved and why don't I walk away?

His kids wanted a relationship with him but found it difficult. They found the courage to talk with me and I respect that. They indicated the things he was doing to me were similar to those he did to their Mother.

Naively I offered to help, thinking he loved me enough to make that leap of faith.

His immediate family saw him as an abuser and mine saw me as a victim. 'Labels' were a thing I understood but by their very nature someone has to break the mould.

It was indicated to me that the problem went back to his grandfather. There's always a story in everyone's family.

I understood, 'learnt hurts' that go deep down and only come out when the wrong buttons are innocently pressed.

But what has that got to do with me? Why all of a sudden do I feel so bad about myself? That was an easy one to answer – I had let Alan in.

Telling him of my past, thinking he would understand, because he professed to be a sensitive soul with similar life experiences.

I was content I didn't need to know too much about his past, unless he wanted to tell me and was happy to answer questions of my own, if it helped to a better understanding. To me love is unconditional................

However, I misjudged Alan's level of understanding, his current behaviour had a direct impact on the present, because it's who we are in the present that is important and how we react to others around us.

Ironically that evening, he rang, and I braced myself for what I knew would be more pain as he quashed the emotions I felt for him. I was expecting a call, we had another counselling session looming but from now on it was only Alan and I. I had removed Grace from the equation, this wasn't her battle.
We went along as usual with Alan bringing up the fact that I slept with someone some years ago, not that it was relevant, other than he is still a friend today and by bringing things up in this way Alan avoided the real issues.
On the way home he began to yell.
> "You should go back to this chap from your past, you belong with either your ex-husband or an ex-boyfriend."
> "But I don't want that Alan, why won't you listen?"
> He didn't stop "You're destroying your daughter. You're abusive. Why won't you just admit it...........................…....…"

I closed off at that point, I saw his lips move but no longer heard their meaning and realised we were in some kind of cycle again.
It continued when we got back so I went straight to my room, unfortunately followed by the irate Alan, who still needed to have the last word and was always right.

After my marriage to Andy, I had a brief affair with a person I had known before I met David. It's hardly a crime, but Alan keeps bringing it up with the counsellor. Is it because he can't bear the thought of there being someone in my past I looked upon as a friend and who helped me like myself? He, unlike Alan never judged and had known my ex-husband even being on the receiving end of his anger, so understood.

However, Grace was unaware of this liason and knew this man as a long-standing friend. So I thanked him for bringing up something that happened years ago, and if I hadn't told him, he would have been none, the wiser. Then asked how he could possibly use this as a weapon against me now.

he seemed completely unabashed and then I realised Grace would have overheard the whole conversation and flipped.

"HOW DARE YOU" I screamed "don't you know the damage you can do. Now I have to explain it to the Grace, you ******* IDIOT. I've fought hard to protect her and all you want to do is ridicule me in front of her. You ******* BASTARD."

"DON'T DO THAT" he screamed.

"Well, I'm hardly going to leave it; with YOUR COMMENTS RINGING IN HER EARS."

"YOU'RE SICK JANE",

"ME!!!!!? HAVE YOU LOOKED IN THE MIRROR LATELY ALAN?"

DON'T DO IT JANE, LEAVE HER OUT OF IT, please."

"YOU SHOULD HAVE THOUGHT ABOUT THAT before you started YELLING at me." I pushed past him, completely enraged by what I saw was a deliberate attempt to cause friction between Grace and myself. I went downstairs towards the kitchen, where I figured Grace had taken refuge.

"Before you jump to any conclusions, just let me explain Grace." She looked at me with revulsion and I knew then the damage was already done and felt my heart sink.

"I don't want to know Mum. Leave me out of it."

"I'm sorry Grace" I said fighting back the tears because I didn't want to lose her now and destroy any glimmer of trust she had left in me, so I took a deep breath and said. "I will tell you, so that you can understand, but not tonight. I'm going to bed now and suggest you do the same."

She gave me one of her half smiles, which meant do you really expect me to sleep and I hugged her.

"Just try, please. I love you very much, always remember that."

I returned to the bedroom but Alan was blocking my way at the top of the stairs, shouting that he needed to do something about me and would call the authorities to have me certified,

"You're a virtual straight jacket job, you really are Jane." He kept saying. "And an abuser. A complete control freak who likes to keep men under your thumb."

I turned and stared at him "If you really believe that stuff then WHY ARE YOU STILL HERE!"

He picked up his things and made his way to the front door still shouting, telling me he would be back with the authorities and rescue Grace.

The following day there was a knock at the door and there he stood.

"You think I'm your ex-husband, don't you?"

"Oh, pleeeeeease Alan, why do you do that?"

I'd always wondered why he referred to the past in arguments, one thing was for sure, he certainly did and said things that reminded me of it, as if he was trying to push me back there! I took a deep breath,

"You seem to understand abuse quite well. Otherwise why would these things matter to you. It's you I've been having a relationship with."

"Look Jane, lets stop tormenting each other with questions."

I nodded and told him I couldn't take much more, it was destroying me,so we decided not to talk for a while and he left on more friendly terms.

A week has flown by and today's the day for the next counselling session, as it has taken days to get over the last one, I'm no longer happy about seeing her.

She had already told me relationships could be difficult but this was heading towards Armageddon. The worrying thing is the self-destruct button that has been pressed in me and I'm on a spiral, whirling out of control, if this is what I am being told is a normal way of life, then this isn't a planet I want to be on for much longer.

Alan's always telling me I don't live in reality, however from my point of view, I'm living it everyday of my life without respite.

I decided to pluck up the courage and mention to the counsellor, what was really happening between sessions as it was beginning to scare me. Alan only refers to previous events during sessions where he feels completely exonerated and gets the counsellor to focus on me, so I suspect she has no idea of what is really happening. I am mindful that he implied that she and he corresponded on an e-mail basis and that I was exhibiting physical conditions which would only make her focus on me more.

But Alan's attention had been drawn away from Grace of late, which has given her time to recuperate and allowed him to focus his attention solely on me. I was comforted by that but worried whether I could cope with the consequences.

I knew he'd be angry if I mentioned anything to the counsellor, he didn't like surprises because he needed to be in control and I could feel the tension it generated and it didn't take long before his anger started to boil over but he kept the lid on till we got into the car.

"YOU'RE A LIAR JANE, YOU'VE MISLED THE COUNSELLOR. YOU'RE AN ABUSER AND A CONTROL FREAK. I'm really going to do something about you now"
His driving became erratic, something else, I was all too familiar with from my past.

"THAT'S IT, YOU NEED TO BE ABUSED." he exclaimed, although my thoughts were ....HELP, I wish I was back in the comfort of my home right now, but I didn't say much, choosing to agree so he would stop driving like a mad man.

On the way he rang his attorney's office in London,

"I need support. My sister will support me, she works for the government, you've chosen the wrong person to mess with, I've got some powerful friends."

I was used to being threatened, used to being told it was 'my fault' and that the authorities didn't want to know.

"Alan, if I've got a problem then I'll look into it but this is hurting me."

"You can start by telling the truth Jane. You're a very cruel person!."

I turned off then, however he continued, talking incessantly till we arrived back at the house, where he dropped me off and sped away. I was glad of the peace and quiet but then there was the inevitable phone call, which I dreaded. Even the sound made me feel sick to the pit of my stomach and Grace had given up answering the phone altogether.

"You've fucked up my life big time Jane. You always want the upper hand, which is abuse. You must have done this with your other relationships. Grace is a big problem. I feel I have been living under a microscope. The counsellor just missed the point. You should really wake up your ideas. You go through life thinking you're perfect. Ask yourself why you do things. You bend the truth and manipulate it in a horrible way. You invent things as if you are living in a fantasy world. You know what you're like deep down and aren't prepared to do anything about it. What have you got to say for yourself? You can't ever admit it and that's why you can't face the things you do. I know it has been rough for you but it doesn't have to be that way. Basically you think I'm wrong all the time, don't you. Why don't you answer?"

"Please Alan, I don't want to talk anymore. It's not a matter of being wrong or right." But he went on......................................

"You start arguments but you are bereft of understanding in certain areas. I'm always building bridges and all you do is break them down to win brownie points. You want me to rubbish myself, and my family to make yourself feel better. I regret what happened in your past but it makes you what you are.
You make me out to be a worse monster than your ex-husband! It is all too much for you isn't it?"
He continued..
"At the counsellor's, it's a forum in which you can say how wonderful you are and how bad I am. You also said you didn't think I mean to cause you any anxiety."

"That's true Alan I don't think you do."
"Well, I look at you as enriched by your life's experiences. This is the way it is. I just want you the way you are. Both of us had less than straightforward lives. We aren't screaming at each other"
(at this point I realised he was right but that's because I wasn't answering back!)
"These are simple domestic problems Jane, we will understand each other, I promise you."

Alan has missed the point, I can't tell him the truth because he doesn't want to hear it. He doesn't want someone in his life like me because I will always have an opinion and he's not ready to accept that right now. As for his family, I accepted his past and am not the one, prying. In fact we talk very little about his family or friends.
I can ignore all the signals but the biggest thing that is destroying me is why?
Alan knew what happened to me and can see the affect this is having on me physically, if he loved me surely he would walk away? But instead he's happy to label both Grace and me.

I feel I'm being pushed back to confront a past, I would rather forget to make Alan feel better because he has already made his mind up as to what the truth really is, irrespective of my view or that of Grace and by doing so has opened up old wounds and all I feel is the pain of guilt. A guilt I have carried around for years, because I was unable to stop Grace from witnessing Andy's behaviour toward me. Mainly because at the time, it was accepted that some men did treat their wives badly and that was their business. 'The rule of Thumb'.

Worse, Allan is systematically destroying all the hard work I have put into moving Grace forward and wants to make me accountable for a past I had no control over.

I on the other hand, needed Grace to believe in one parent at least and yet Alan is hell-bent on destroying the very foundations of her life and I feel powerless to stop it. I have no where to run, nowhere to hide, it's wholly my fault and I'm wholly to blame that's the society I was brought up in but it wasn't what I wanted for Grace so Alan can destroy me all he likes but Grace still needs a family around her.

Alan continued, this time ridiculing the counsellor.

> "She's incompetent, I have a good mind to do something about her. I'm just the victim in all this, Jane. I DON'T KNOW WHY YOU DON'T WANT TO ADMIT IT, YOU'RE AN ABUSER AND THAT'S THAT. It's very clear. You don't even get phone calls at home because everyone knows what you're like."

He had a point, but they didn't ring because they thought by doing so, it would make matters worse. I imagined Alan at the other end of the phone, veins throbbing in his head, his face red with rage, spitting out the words. Frantically trying to work out what I was thinking to make sure he could prove me wrong and make me feel it's all, my fault.

> "JANE, he screamed, WHAT HAVE YOU GOT TO SAY FOR YOURSELF."
>
> "Nothing, you're doing all the talking and the person you're referring to is not a pretty sight. Why don't we call it a day. Don't forget Grace and I have accepted your family's past, but for whatever reason, you are unable to accept ours."

Alan put the phone down.

The following morning I got up to find Grace had written a note: **'Mum, I've had enough of this, I can't take anymore, I'll give you one month to sort this out. This is constant abuse towards you and me. I'm too young to have my brains fucked in by a serial abuser and watch you slowly die as your life draws from you as he knocks you down. I'm seriously considering leaving. You are in denial that abuse is love and settling for what you think you deserve. You don't trust each other in your relationship and I don't want to be involved. You can fight each other to death but you can't deny that you aren't meant to be together.'**

She was right, of course! Alan was unable to take ownership of his problem and whatever deep emotional bond, had developed between us, was now destroying us. No one is the winner in this. It has hurt us all and further damaged the relationship I had with Grace.

Robin rang and I found myself sobbing down the phone telling him of my plight.

> "Jane, I've never heard you speak like this, you sound so upset. From what you're saying Alan's not being straightforward, I suggest you make a note of all his business dealings, something is very amiss here and if you're not careful you'll get caught up in it."
> "But he just seems to have an anger issue Robin."
> "Look Jane take it from me, there's more to it than that, just safe guard yourself, I don't trust him. I strongly advise you to cover yourself, there is more to Alan than meets the eye. Make sure you do it for you and Grace. Promise me Jane, just do it."
> "OK, well I haven't seen him for a while so maybe that's it."
> "It won't be Jane, he's a certain type. Just TRUST me on it. I've got to go now, be strong. I'll speak with you soon."

I made another note on my laptop…………..

> **Anger begins with folly, and ends with repentance, Pythagoras**
> **Man creates the evil he endures, Robert Southey**

That's a big one for me, TRUST, there are few people I trust anymore but I followed Robin's advice.

Robin was right Alan did come back and the relationship drifted on with highs and lows, Alan refusing to let go, wanting to be a friend one minute, reaching part way with his emotions and then backtracking. Eventually through a spurious set of events the inevitable happened. A weekend away intended to remove any doubts on either side turned into yet another disaster. It started well, Alan wanted to look at property in Ilfracombe, Devon, suggesting we move away and start afresh. He took down the number of an estate agent and asked me to ring them so we could view a couple of properties but on the return journey, he began again, going on about my past. This time pursuing a course, of threatening to ring David, still hot on the trail of finding proof of my abuse, driving erratically and slamming on the brakes to frighten me into submission.

> "I've already spoken to Andy and he tells me he never touched you. I know where David lives, so I'm going to ring directory

enquiries", which is exactly what he did, only to find he was ex-directory. And I was amazed because the last I had heard of David was that he had gone to live in Africa.

"I bet he's got some stories to tell about you". Continued Alan.

"I'm going to get to the bottom of this and I'm going to prove your book is based on lies"

All I wanted was for him to stop tormenting me with a past I want to forget. I screamed at him to stop the car, as the seat-belt cut accross my chest.

"OK, you can get out and I'm going to leave you here, give me back your shoes, I paid for them and I'll have the mobile as well, now GET OUT! I wish I'd never set eyes on you, you will pay for what you've done"

I did as he asked, throwing the shoes onto the back seat and handing over the mobile phone. He looked at me in disgust "GET OUT", he screamed and I heard the screech of the tyres as he drove away, leaving me in a narrow lane somewhere near Taunton,in Somerset and approximately 200 miles from home. I tried to flag down a passing motorist, who had to swerve to avoid me. In the distance I saw another car had already stopped, a small white metro. But just as I was about to walk across to the waiting vehicle, Alan returned, jumped out and tried to 'man-handle' me back into his car, I slipped his clutches and ran towards the parked vehicle, a woman sat in the drivers seat,

"Looks like you're in trouble, jump in". She drove off with Alan in pursuit. "You look pretty shaken up, I used to have a problem with a man, namely my father". She said. "You know he's following us don't you?" I looked into the sideview mirror and could see an irate Alan looming up behind. "What do you want me to do?" She enquired.

"Pull over, maybe he will pass".

She did as I asked but Alan stopped just in front, getting out and taking my luggage and shoes from the back of the car and putting them on the ground. I nipped out, grabbed my belongings and jumped back into the car and he waited whilst we drove away. He kept the mobile though,so I couldn't make any calls. He was always worried about me ringing people. On route the women who called herself Geraldine told me she had run retreats for battered women, she had jotted her details on the back of a card, which I slipped into my pocket. I remember how well dressed she was for that time of day, as it was still early afternoon. She told me she was visiting a male friend who lived in East Dulwich, London, an area I knew vaguely and hoped to make it from there to my mother's home. Geraldine also very kindly let me to use her phone to ring Grace, who was unwell. She told me she hadn't heard from Alan and asked if he was having some sort of breakdown.

"I don't know sweetheart, I am ringing from someone's phone right now so I'll keep this short. I will try and get back tonight but no guarantees, I don't have any cash with me, so I may have to stay at mum's"

"Take care, I love you mum."

"I love you too darling."

I was intrigued that Geraldine had run a refuge for abused women. She told me that she had problems with her father, and although had never really suffered abuse herself but was happy to help others. She seemed pleasant enough and I felt quite pleased here was someone I could relate to. We chatted most of the way and before long had arrived in Dulwich. I thanked her and promised to keep in touch to send her some money and flowers for her trouble.

I walked off in a direction I felt would lead to somewhere I was more familiar with and on seeing a phone box, took a twenty pence piece from my bag and rang Grace to tell her I had arrived in London but wouldn't be able to call her again as that was all the money I had with me. It was around 7.30pm and was beginning to get dark, I knew I wouldn't make it back without help and then I spotted a police station. I went inside and explained my predicament. They were great, organising a taxi, which took me to my mother's home, unfortunately she was out but a neighbour took me in and from there I organised another taxi back home, arriving around midnight. Grace was so relieved and had just began to tell me about Alan, who arrived at around the same time as I telephoned from the phone box, when suddenly there was a knock at the door, which made us both jump. Warily, I opened it to find two police officers standing on the doorstep.

"We are looking for Alan Sedgewick."

"He's not here" I said, "You'll probably find him at his flat, if not, I don't know where he is."

"So he doesn't live here?"

"No, what's this all about?"

"I'm afraid it is a matter we need to discuss with him. When will he be back?"

"I don't know you'll probably find him at the flat, as I said"

"Can you tell us where that is?"

"Yes, it umm, it's a few miles off Brackens Road, I don't know the exact address but I can give you the name of the lady he rents from. What's this all about? "

"It's regarding a missing person"

106

"Oh", I sighed "that doesn't happen to be me does it?"

"And your name is?"

"Jane Howard"

The officers looked at each other. "Can we come in?"

"Yes, sure, I've just got in myself, it's been a long day."

It appeared Alan, having returned home, decided to call the police and report me as a 'missing person'. Grace confirmed that Alan had popped in briefly before going, presumably back to his flat.

"We understand you're writing a book." One of the officers said.

"Who told you that?" I said in amazement.

"Are you writing a book?"

"Well, I wrote one sometime ago, over a number of years. But what's that got to do with anything?"

"Can we see it?"

"Umm, sure, I've got a copy round here somewhere."

I went upstairs to look for the manuscript, returning to find them speaking with Grace.

"Here it is." I said, handing over the copy and watched whilst they flicked through the pages.

"Has Alan read this?"

"He read one chapter but didn't like what he read, so I didn't let him read anymore."

"And why do you think that is?"

"I really haven't a clue, it didn't have anything to do with him."

"You would think he would have supported you on it"

"Yeah, I didn't understand that either."

I took the card from my pocket and handed it to the officer.

"This is the lady who picked me up after Alan dropped me in the middle of nowhere."

The officer looked at it and handed it back

"That won't help us", he said.

"But you can call her, she'll verify everything I have said!!, just give her a call."

The two officers looked at each other and then handed me a leaflet on domestic violence.

"Ring the number for the domestic violence unit, they'll be able to help. You've been very lucky, anything could have happened to you but you probably did the best thing by getting out of the car. Do call the number. Years ago we may not have taken these things seriously but we do now."

I thanked them and showed them out.

"What do I do now Grace?"

"Call the number, it can't do any harm Mum." Puzzled, bewildered and tired, I looked at the card Geraldine had given me, she had written her details on the back of an estate agents card, funnily enough the one Alan had asked me to phone over our weekend in Ilfracombe. However, I had a restless night, I was worried about Grace, who was worried about me and worried about what the hell was happening around us. The following day I rang the number given to me by the police and then the number Geraldine has written down, which didn't exist. Her address read 22 Soho, Leigh upon Mendip, BA3 5RD. Her email geraldine@soho22.fsnet.co.uk, didn't exist either. Well I suppose that makes it clear, she just didn't want to get involved.

But from here on, I wasn't alone and by meeting with the domestic violence unit, I began for the first time in my life to understand the meaning of psychological abuse. I'd been through a violent relationship where there was no-one to help and thought psychological torture was something you put up with. 'Sticks and stones may break my bones but names will never hurt me' but they do, they hurt a lot. Unfortunately you think they won't get into your subconscious but it was the emotional damage that was hardest to come to terms with.

By distancing myself from it I began to find strength. Alan returned into my life only now I felt I had the support around me. Unfortunately, I still had issues trusting the police, especially as Alan had hinted of his contacts there. One was a Doctor who worked with the Police and was an apparent computer genius, who fallen under suspicion of molesting young boys. Alan didn't believe the charges and thought him too clever to be found guilty, so I got a copy of my medical records for safe keeping. Another story Alan told me, was that of a solicitor friend who had just been found guilty of misusing clients funds, when she became incapable of handling her own affairs. 'I have a friend whose father is in the House of Lords', Alan had said 'so you are not going to get very far with your lies. You've heard the expression 'Lamb to slaughter' and you know the solicitors indemnity fund is broke, don't you?'

I didn't understand any of it but was frightened about what I was hearing. Eventually the Police surgeon, having been arrested was jailed for sex attacks on young girls, not boys as Alan had told me. It appeared he preyed upon his friends children, which send a chiver down my spine.

The final straw for me came when Alan appeared on the doorstep, irate about a phone call he had made earlier in the day. A neighbour had popped in for coffee and had been with me most of the day and as neither of us had heard the phone ring, I was bemused by Alan's insistence of a phone call he had made to the house and rang the phone myself from my mobile to see if it was working. Alan, still enraged, stormed over to the phone, dialling 1471 to prove he made the call. But now it registered my mobile, which enraged him further and he strode from the house, screaming that I was mad.

As my normal 'modus operandi' at these times was to buy yet another packet of cigarettes, I walked the short distance to the local pub, returning to find Alan once again on the doorstep.

"Please leave me alone. I don't understand any of this and I just want to be on my own."

"You'd like that wouldn't you? But you can't get away with this, dealing with people like you do. I know you have done it before. That's what women do, but you won't get away with it. I'm going to prove my innocence. You've been abusing your daughter for years."

"I don't know what you mean Alan?"

"Oh yes you do and now you think you can take everything out on me. You are abusing me just like you abused the other men in your life and your daughter. The counsellor knows it's you, we all do. Even the police asked if there was any mental instability in the family, remember? You didn't know that did you?"

He was wrong, he had already mentioned it to me but I let him carry on.

"Well you know the policeman that came round when your abusive friend rang. You know the one you used to work with. There's a story there, I can tell you. Well that's when he told me and he's right. Look what you've just done you rang your own number, that's not normal behaviour."

I tired in vain telling him what happened but it just made him worse and he started strutting round the house, shouting at me that I was in denial of being an abuser and that society needed protecting from me.

"People rely on me Jane, I've got a business to run and look at yourself, why can't you just admit it, no one is going to think too badly of you. You can't help yourself but you brought it upon yourself. All this smoking yourself to death, you're doing it to yourself, it's you but you just can't face it, you can't face who you really are. You're rude, abusive, even your daughter is abusive. I've lived here a long time and I've lots of friends in the area, do you think for one moment my integrity is in doubt? I was married 25 years, albeit to a women I never loved, but we brought up two normal children but look at your daughter, she's rude, arrogant and I bet I know where she gets it from."

Alan's face went white and he strode off, in search for something, not waiting to see what he returned with, I locked my self in the downstairs loo and telephoned the police. I could feel my body shaking and to my astonishment, within a short period of time, four officers arrived and asked him to leave.

Of course he was back the following day, an officer in tow, as I hadn't been answering his calls. Eventually I opened the door, having been unable to sleep, I just wanted was to be left alone. Accompanied by the officer he insisted he wished to collect more of his things, making comment about women as he walked around, eventually leaving and ringing later to say he had told the officer I was at risk of committing suicide out of guilt.

I rang the counsellor and on her advice, rang Alan telling him I was terminating the relationship unless he addressed his anger and got help and that from now on he go for counselling alone.

Surprisingly, he did just that and for a few months things quietened down and I really thought he was making progress. However, Alan's sole motivation was only to prove his innocence of some wrong doing, culminating in a series of verbal attacks whereby he tried to force me to apologise to the police for wasting their time. But I refused to co-operate, because this time it was me that was in control. I was still reading a book recommended by the counsellor, which Alan had shown no interest in and continued to call 'socialist bullshit'. However, I needed to understand what was happening.

My lack of co-operation, unfortunately sent Alan through a really bad patch, where he would call, saying he was contemplating his own suicide. At one point asking to meet because he could no longer cope and then forcing my hand onto the handle of a bread knife, whilst he pressed the other end to his stomach, inflicting bruising as I struggled to free my hands.

So Alan now had to face his own demons but I listened, encouraging him to do something about these feelings and told him I would be there for him.

I rang the counsellor who felt he had an issue with women and that maybe a male colleague would be able to help and Alan attended regularly every week.

110

Chapter 6

What's really happening here

I went back to my laptop.......................... By accusing me of things Alan was controlling me, making me feel guilty about my past, accusing me of infidelity or flirting, when it was probably the reverse. He used unassailable logic extremely convincing to those around him and likely to deceive many people. He was so convincing that at times you just got mesmerised.

Abuse is a gradual process. You think you can change them but they will always make you feel it is your fault. Psychological abuse is the worst form of abuse, leading to low self-esteem and loss of confidence. You neglect yourself and put other people first.

Abusers are bullies - they think they own you lock, stock and barrel and put in control mechanisms to keep you that way. They pick on women they regard as having low self-esteem, usually women in need or with children to support. If you had the time to analyse it, it's called 'blame transference'. Often it is they that have low self-esteem. But for you it will lead to chronic insecurity.

I seldom go out of the house now, it's like being brainwashed and the person I was, is not the person I have become. Alan, on the other hand has bought yet another house and I can't be sure but I think he is also seeing someone else. He's already moved four times since we've known each other, finally buying a home that he wants Grace and I to share with him. Grace however, doesn't want to know, but Alan seems confident she'll change her mind as for me, well I'm just waiting for the next eruption and in the meantime, I'm writing a book.

Typical scenario: Successful career and just want the 'little woman' at home to blame when things go wrong. Men often feel trapped into getting married and then feel burdened by the upbringing of children. At the same time men play the 'power and politics' game and like to have a woman on their arm they can parade as an asset or even the 'Trophy'.

The 'little woman' at home wants to bring up and nurture the children of the marriage and the man wants to keep her that way, often by isolating her. When isolation is complete, they have total control.

Not being able to compete in the 'power and politics' game you become full of guilt, too paralysed or trapped to escape.

The thing that draws you back to abuse is the emotional hole that has been made inside you. An emptiness, you feel only the abuser can fill, (better the devil you know syndrome) but all they want is to make the hole bigger. That is the malignant part of you, you feel you can't control, like a drug. By removing the drug, the hole gradually begins to heal, but you need to be out of the situation before you can start analysing it. The easiest thing is to run away, although we all know that financial restraints and children prevent many from doing so.

I'm deeply saddened to say Alan sees only an injustice perpetrated against him and he is the only victim. We have spent some wonderful times together and he is learning to control the other side by taking 'time out'. That means walking away from confrontation and not allowing it to become abusive, but we both know it isn't working. And after a recent row with Grace, he has come full circle, accusing her of being the abuser and labelling both of us as damaged goods, protecting his own family from the scrutiny of others and ladling us with guilt, convenient, isn't it?
What he didn't realise was that we had no interest in analysing his past, everyone has a story to tell. We just wanted to move forward with our lives but by his actions, he was keeping us firmly tied to a past we desperately wanted to leave behind.
Grace told me how hurt she has been after Alan refused to hear how she felt as a child and how she was angered by his accusation of abuse towards him. His final comments to her were, by text on her mobile, telling her to never contact him or his family again and to stay away from his children. But that didn't matter anymore, she is an individual in her own right and all Alan was doing was projecting his own pain, by trying to control the actions of others around him.
By being brave you become part of the denial conspiracy. The problem with Psychological abuse is proving it, even to the abuser, as he always has an explanation for his behaviour and easily hides or justifies his abuse and will go to great lengths to prove it's you.
Nothing you can do, can alter an abuser's behaviour. Only they can do that by recognising it!

'He that is without sin among you, let him cast a stone at her' St. John chapter 8 verse 7

Intellect is invisible to the man who has none, Arthur Schopenhauer

Throughout all of this my daughter, of whom I am extremely proud, remained steadfast in her love and devotion, which has enabled me to carry on. She searched the Internet for relevant topics, and kept me focused to stop me from completely 'self-destructing'.

So, for her, and children/ young adults like her; I trust this it will prove a useful weapon against abuse.
A useful tool to form an understanding and stop them repeating the pattern.
For those struggling to come to terms with abuse, like me, you don't / didn't deserve it, and it's not your fault

I was once asked to put my life into 5 chapters, didn't quite manage it, so to end, here is someone that did:

An Autobiography

In Five Chapters

Chapter 1
I walk down the street
There is a deep hole in the sidewalk
I fall in......
I am lost......I am helpless
But it isn't my fault
But it takes forever to find a way out

Chapter 2
I walk down the same street
There is a deep hole in the sidewalk
I pretend I don't see it
I fall in again
I can't believe I am in the same place
It isn't my fault
But it still takes a long time to get out

Chapter 3
I walk down the same street
There is a deep hole in the sidewalk
I see its there
I fall in.....it's a habit....but now my eyes
are open
It is my fault
I get out immediately

Chapter 4
I walk down the street
There is a deep hole in the sidewalk
I walk around it

Chapter 5
I walk down a different street

Author unknown.

There is a lot going on in the world today. Anger is everywhere, so maybe we should start asking the question why? The lessons should start at home and in the classroom.

The cosmopolitan society we find ourselves living in brings with it, it's own problems. It is right we should start looking at the fundamentals of our society. Parenting should be taught at school.

With an increase in street crime, and a growing threat of terrorism looming, it's not such a bad thing to start looking at the issues of domestic violence. There are some very vulnerable young people coming out of these families that, if they don't understand what's happening, may fall prey to the criminal element or political activist groups.

If you thought this was the end of the story you were wrong; I didn't run away, after all Grace is now twenty-one. Unfortunately, I couldn't give her quite the home life I had wanted for her.

Instead for a treat, I took her up in a hot air balloon. She had always been frightened of heights since an incident in her childhood and this was my way of helping her gently face that issue and getting her to look at the bigger picture.
The views were breathtaking, an exhilarating experience she will always

remember. Being above the problem, was my way of demonstrating to her that, the world is still, a beautiful place.
She now works as a child practitioner and recently underwent an intensive training course on child abuse and I was there to support her.

Alan, well he has continued with counselling, however, on his last visit, to which I was also asked to attend, he maintained he had been abused by me for the last few years and subsequently joined the male abuse support group. Later telling me he would claim he did so in support of my work. However, he's never let me read the paperwork he received and on our last meeting, was reading a document, a Law Commission Consultation paper 173 entitled 'partial defences to murder'.

> "I am going to do something about you Jane," He said, "I know a lot of powerful people. I have even been invited to the House of Lords for a charity dinner, dealing with mentally disturbed people. You will be sorry you ever crossed me."

And that's where I left him, I already knew he was seeing someone else I could feel it which made a nonsense of the counselling sessions and I rang the counsellsor to say so.

For me, not only was Alan not part of the 20%, the whole process was the worst emotional experience of my life, and as for Grace.................

All I can do is trust this goes part way to understanding a complex subject and my advice is, don't suffer alone, the police are there to help.

I turned on the radio, it was playing a song by Craig David entitled 'I'm walking away from the troubles in my life' which seemed appropriate.

My voice has been silenced all these years because it didn't matter. Now I am not afraid to say what I think, silence has no place in my world, my thoughts will always be my own and my spirit will always be free.
If you bond with truth, your consciousness is free of the mental barrier. The deeper this permeates your consciousness, the clearer it becomes.

	YES	NO
Here are some tips for recognising the Wrong person **Do the following:** **Go through the list and tick YES or No to all statements that refer to the person in question**		
Never wants to think about his own behaviour and motives		
Is insensitive about your sexual needs		
Is friendly to you in the presence of others but humiliates you when you are alone		
Humiliates you in public		
Is secretly unfaithful		
Has extreme changes of humour		
Always blames other people in situations		
After a quarrel, acts as if nothing has happened		
Always walks away when you want to talk about the problems between the two of you		
Is excessively jealous of the time you spend with others, including the children		
Demands that you give things up for him		
Is known to others as an unpleasant person		
Is aggressive, false and sadistic towards animals		
Hasn't furnished his home		
Doesn't take good care of himself		

116

	YES	NO
Never does anything for you by himself		
Overloads you with presents and expensive gifts		
Is mean with his money and expects things in return		
Never buys you a birthday present		
Always wants to pay for everything for you		
Always lets you pay		
Doesn't talk to you for days		
Disappears for days and doesn't tell you where he's been		
Shows no real interest in you or what you are doing		
Submits you to an examination of former relationships		
Makes racist and discriminating comments		
Makes sexually slanted and vulgar jokes		
Watches sex programs on TV and visits sex sites on the Internet		
Knows the whereabouts of local brothels		
Takes more than he gives, emotionally		
Possesses hard porno magazines and videotapes		

	YES	NO
Has a fundamental opinion		
Demands all the attention for himself		
Is jealous about your capabilities and is never happy with your success and never gives you compliments		
Is never tender, affectionate and loving		
Gives too much love and affection but in a false way		
Doesn't stimulate you to develop yourself		
Prefers to make you feel small and keep you that way		
Has no family contacts and doesn't maintain them		
Is loyal to suspicious friends or has hardly any friends		
Is unfriendly towards his children and neglects them		
Does most of the talking and talks only about him		
Shows swanky behaviour and doesn't acknowledge the part others may play		
Has no consideration of others		
Always at first puts lots of food on his plate, irrespective if there is enough for others		
Only does something for others if he gets something in return		

	YES	NO
Wants to be your 'saviour'		
Never keeps an agreement		
Always chooses for himself and never for you		
Talks in a nice way but never makes anything concrete		
Heads for sex quickly		
During sex doesn't use a condom		
Is on the phone a lot and always demonstrates how popular he is		
Threatens, blackmails and manipulates		
Is involved in criminal activities or a judicial past		
Doesn't show up for weeks then turns up on your doorstep		
Is not clear about his feelings for you, always changing his mind		
Doesn't remember anything that is important to you		
Works 60 – 80 hours a week		
From day one he wants to share all his traumas and bad experiences with you		
Tells vague and contradicting stories		

	YES	NO
Never asks your opinion or advice		
Always denies his feelings		
Is very fond of children and is very "sticky" and "physical" towards children		
Always talks about his mother		
Leaves the household to you		
Always criticises others		
Always complains and never sees his faults		
Is involved in many lawsuits		
Is a very bad loser		
Doesn't learn from his mistakes and repeats them		
Humiliates you in a sexual way		
Forces sexual activities on you		
Is often picking quarrels		
During quarrels calls you names, whore, slapper, slut or bitch		
Denies you love, sex, money and attention out of revenge		
Controls everything you say and do		
Always criticises you		
Can't be alone		

	YES	NO
Threatens to break up the relationship when you don't do what he wants		
Treats your feelings as hysterical behaviour		
Always decides how often and when you will see each other		
Spends a lot of money, even when he can't afford it		
Never gives money to charity		
Behaves impudently, unfriendly and indecent in front of other people		
Is violent		
Is an aggressive driver		
Often drinks too much		
Drives after drinking		
After a party always wants you to drive		
Has an addiction		
Is insistent on sex in bed and doesn't take no for an answer		
Shows very seductive behaviour		
Very quickly after first meeting, becomes impertinent		
Lies and deceives frequently		
Always is in denial		

	YES	NO
Treats you and others without due respect		
Has a split life, dual personality		
Leaves a trail of broken hearts behind him		
Gets into debt		
Is aloof, arrogant and excessive and demonstrates inflexible behaviour		
Is jealous and possessive		

If there are too many yes's in the above list, you need to:
BREAK FREE

REMEMBER: -
1. IT'S NOT YOU
2. MAKE A PLAN AND STICK TO IT
3. GET THE CHILDREN OUT
4. UNDERSTAND IT'S JUST THE WAY THEY ARE PROGRAMMED TO THINK

IF YOU STILL HAVE DOUBTS, GO THROUGH THIS SHORT CHECK LIST:	YES
Tick the boxes	
DO THEY RESPECT YOU	
DO THEY LISTEN TO YOU	
ARE THEY PHYSICAL WITH YOU	
DO YOU SUFFER HEADACHES	
ARE YOU CONSTANTLY TIRED	

	YES
DO THEY CALL YOU NAMES	
DO THEY TELL YOU IT'S ALWAYS YOUR FAULT	

NOTES

1. This list is not the result of scientific research neither is it complete, you can fill it in further with the help of some friends
2. The potential candidate should be observed for a while because first impressions can be wrong
3. Men who score badly on the checklist are probably unsuitable partners.
4. Never show this list to a new candidate. He will alter his behaviour to become socially acceptable.
5. Hide this book and checklist before he arrives.
6. Be honest, ask yourself how you would answer the checklist.
7. Introduce him to some good friends and let them judge him according to the list. You maybe dazzled by his charm and unable to make a proper judgement
8. If he scores on several points, don't think you are making a mistake and that he will change.
9. Don't start a new educational, development and caring project. When he scores high on your list, just let him go
10. Keep comfort in the thought that nice, caring, inspiring, intelligent, cheerful, attractive, with integrity, honesty, and with potential, but above all reliable men, **DO EXIST**, and they will come to you.
11. It may take a while but they will surely come your way.

ABOVE ALL REMEMBER, IF HE IS THE WRONG PERSON FOR YOU - IT IS NOT YOUR FAULT AND YOU ARE NOT TO BLAME

Chapter 7

Profile of an abuser

-Charming, makes demands seem romantic to the
exclusion of others
-Isolates you from your family and friends
-You must be the focus of his attention
-Any attempt by a third party to share your love and attention is
  viewed as a threat
-Is the one in control
-You must devote your time and energy to him alone
-Makes all the plans and the rules
-Friends are criticised and actively discouraged
-Only his friends and their views count
-Ridicules you
-Humiliates you in public
-Makes you feel inadequate and incapable of holding down a
job
- Accuses you of deserting the children or of being a bad
  mother
-Needs to know where you are and who you are with
-Is over-possessive and jealous
-Accuses you of being unfaithful
-Actively discourages friends or activities outside the home
-Uses his temper as a controlling mechanism
-Says he suffers from low self esteem and feels insecure.
-His fears and emotions are masked by controlling and
  abusive behaviour
-Is inadequate and worthless but cannot admit it.
-Is frightened of real intimacy and feels the need to
  control
-Prefers to seek out women with low self esteem because
they are easier to control and dominate
-Will always have the last say and always needs to
  win in any confrontation
-Is never wrong
-It is always your fault
-If he can't get through by intimidation tactics, he uses the
  guise of helping, acting as your therapist or teacher
-Has macho ideals of manhood

-Substance abuse problems
-Abusive childhood
-Is in denial

All abusers feel that women are weak and need to be dominated.
Due to their low-self-esteem, this feeds their need to dominate and is the only way they feel better about themselves
It is 'learnt behaviour' from either trauma, a poor role model or having been witness to abuse in childhood.
They lack the ability to accept responsibility for their own actions.
In general, abuse is carried out in a cycle. Attack, pull you in, be nice, attack again, be understanding, pull you in further. Good guy, bad guy routine. This is often why women stay in the cycle for so long.

Your part in the profile

Co-dependency

Many Psychologists argue this dependency is created at infancy, when the child is nourished, encouraged, loved and protected by its mother, and feels panicky and insecure when ignored. So the need to fulfil the mother role goes on into adulthood.

The way I see it is that you want a partner in your life you can rely on. Most of us want a mate and there is nothing wrong in that and we also want someone we can depend upon. However co-dependency is when you believe you cannot survive without your partner.

And you become co-dependent when you become chronically insecure and suffer from low self esteem and that is the way an abuser makes you feel. When you fight back it becomes a game because you attack the abusers vulnerabilities that they try desperately to cover up, hence co-dependency. Partners of abusers experience denial of the abusive behaviour, similar to denial experienced by addicts and just as life threatening. The abused partner will often remain loyal to the abuser until the denial is broken.

Chemical dependency for both partners is common and often acts as another form of control. Isolation provides an ideal ground for the abuser to encourage chemical dependency, which can lead to addiction.

When you have failed to get him to understand, you are left with the pain of what you put yourself through and the guilt of failure.

Many women start with high self esteem, which is systematically broken, when they fall in love with an abuser, who sets out to humiliate and undermine them to the point where they believe it. When the abuser then tells them they are bad, mad, crazy or that it is their fault that men behave towards them in that way, the emotional abuse they suffer cuts to the core, creating deep scars lasting longer than physical ones. With the constant insults, insinuations, criticism and accusations eating away at the victim, they become incapable of realistically judging a situation and blame themself for the abuse and cling closer to the abuser for reassurance of that fact.

The abuser is dependent on the woman because this gives him a sense of power.
So he plays a game and you unwittingly join in and the more you try and pull away the more he enjoys the challenge. It becomes a battle of wills – HIS WILL.

Making excuses for his behaviour

-He tells you he is under stress
-What about the stress you are suffering?
-He cannot control himself
-He does because he is in control
-Immediately after abuse he is able to turn on the charm to convince neighbours and friends and police that you are just exaggerating things.
-He is the breadwinner
-What part do you play?

Non abusers

Many men who are under stress DO NOT ABUSE THEIR WIVES/PARTNERS

Many men suffer from low self esteem but DO NOT ABUSE THEIR WIVES/PARTNERS

A woman cannot make a man abusive IT IS ALWAYS HIS CHOICE

For interest, here is an extract from a book written in 1853 on correct conduct

It was intended as a guide and mentor in the important affairs in Life.

'It is certain that he who lives correctly everyday will find himself following the higher laws of morality and rectitude. As a preceptor for young and old alike, it will be found invaluable, giving as it does the rules to be observed by children in their conduct towards their parents, and the duties of parents towards their children.'

Here are some interesting points:

For a man to consider that money spent to give pleasure to his wife and family is money well spent'.

'For women of the household to make it pleasant and attractive, and for the men to show their appreciation of these efforts'

'To remember that the lady who rules the household must have absolute authority in it and rule as absolute queen. No comfort or order can be obtained without this. If her orders are questioned, the correct thing is to do so in private, and never in the presence of the young members of the household'.

'For the lady who holds this position to remember that the every-day happiness of those in the home circle is in her hands'.

'To imagine that little quarrels, or unpleasant discussions over small matters, are of no consequence. Too often they alienate those who loved each other as time goes on, and frequently drive those who are free to leave it from a home in which they would otherwise be happy'.

'To marry for love; and if you have not done so, to treat your wife with the same courtesy and gentleness as though you had, both before others and when alone'.

'To study to please her in all such matters that do not involve a question of right and wrong'.

'To guard her; not as a slave, by tyranny or harshness, but like a jewel, with care and forethought'.

'To establish, in every-day life, a system of "give and take."

'It is not the correct thing – to storm and scold if dinner is five minutes late'

'It is not the correct thing - Some men think it right to treat their wives as inferiors'

'It is the correct thing – for parents and children to be good friends'

Society's part

Marriage

"Who giveth this woman?" the question that is asked in the traditional Church of England wedding service which goes on to demand that she 'love, honour and obey' her husband 'For better or for worse'.

Abusers hold onto this belief going on to view you as their property, an asset or trophy.

Tradition views men as the dominant sex. They are the head of the family, the breadwinner and by these very attitudes we give abusers the power and control they require.

Historically women were chattels, unable to own property. No rights in law.

Until recently could not be raped by their husband.

Tradition plays a part by branding you as inferior to men.

By giving men the more dominant role by the institution of marriage, women become trapped. Forced to give up careers in order to bring up children and become financially dependent on their husbands/ partners - 'The poverty trap'.

Women often sacrifice their own lives to support this belief, taking menial jobs to help their men develop and sometimes these men walk out on the family leaving the woman feeling chronically insecure and vulnerable.

The Koran gives a similar message that 'Men are the managers of the affairs of women'

Between the 15th and 18th centuries some nine million women were accused of being witches because they challenged men's authority and many were burned at the stake.

We are encouraged to nurture men towards power and success.

With all these messages, it's no wonder we get confused. However it is down to the individuals concerned to form a good marriage or partnership, we all know the difference between right and wrong and when we are making others unhappy.

For society to consider

If you think someone may be suffering from domestic violence. Get hold of a leaflet, they are freely available at doctors surgerys throughout the country and discreetly pop it through the door.
We live in a judgmental society but don't naturally assume a person with an abusive past enjoys it, or that they are any different from you or me.
Here are a few stories we can all relate to:
An ex-war veteran in his late 70's was looking after his eight-year old grandson and was soon exhausted, falling asleep in the chair. The child, realising granddad was resting, decided to surprise him, and threw his arms around his neck in order to place a kiss on his cheek. The ex-commando woke with a start, grabbing the child and throwing him over his shoulder.
Realising to his horror what he had done he clutched his grandson to his chest. "I'm so sorry," he sobbed. "Are you alright, oh what have I done?" "Yes, Grandad", cried the frightened child. "Thank God, thank God. I just get a little nervous when people creep up on me like that. I never mean't to harm you, are you sure you are alright?" The child nodded. "I'm not going to fall asleep again, let's go and play in the garden" The child was soon pacified as Grandad reassured him of his love.

Later, the veteran phoned a friend. "The most awful thing happened today, I was looking after my grandchild and fell asleep in the chair. The next thing I recall was an arm round my neck and for a moment there, I, well, I grabbed the arm and didn't realise it was my grandson just trying to give me a kiss. Can you imagine that, I feel so dreadful, I could have killed him." "Is he alright?", his friend asked. "He must have been terrified." "He was but he's fine now, it's just, oh what have I done." "Pull yourself together man, everything's alright. I've been there myself, it's just the way we've been trained to react but you're not there anymore. Nothing happened and it wouldn't have happened you're too strong-minded. The people you refer to in society are weak minded, bullies. You were trained to kill in the line of duty, kill or be killed remember but not women or children. I've known you too long to think ill of you. You're a kind and compassionate man, don't concern yourself with imaginings."

Still shaken by the ordeal he spoke with his family about what happened. His son, was at first angry. "I'm really sorry son, I have no defence, it was my fault, I should never have fallen asleep and if you decide not to let me see my grandson in future, I'd quite understand." "Dad, we love you, and your past was a long time ago, so let's leave it there. Just promise me you won't fall asleep again." "Oh, I promise, son. I really promise." He said as tears rolled down his cheeks and his son hugged him. "It's OK Dad," I understand.
****

A woman librarian in her forties. At the age of five, was sexually abused by her father, it continued into her mid teens. Accepting this as normal behaviour, she also slept around and was used my men. When she was fourteen, a neighbour invited her to his home, thinking this was just another invite into bed, she accepted. However, something she said made the neighbour question her behaviour and ask if she had been abused as a child. It was the first time anyone had asked her, so she spoke about her past and as a result, he decided to take some action and phoned the police. Her father was arrested, however the family were far from understanding. She was shunned, labelled and ostracised as if she had some part to play and fell into the perpetual victim syndrome, innocent of any crime but judged by society.
It took 15 years of therapy for her to come to terms with what happened. She now works as a counsellor.
****

Male council worker late thirties. Mother was an alcoholic and introduced him to alcohol at the age of eight. She eventually died as a

result of her drinking. He worked long hours, drank incessantly, was aware of his mother's influence and felt he was controlling the habit but eventually it controlled him. He found it difficult to accept he had a problem even when others pointed it out to him, eventually he lost his job because he couldn't break the pattern given to him as a child.
****

Advertising salesman late thirties. Mother died when he was eight, so father had a big influence on his life.

Father was an alcoholic and introduced the child to the betting office when he was young. As he grew he wanted to better himself, was career minded and achieved his goals by the age of twenty-six. The drawback was that he had become a compulsive gambler. Eventually he gambled more than he had and lost everything. Still not convinced he had a problem he began gambling with other people's money. He only addressed the problem, after taking money from his employer's safe to place on a sure bet and lost. He couldn't hide the fact that the money was missing, so had no choice but to admit to taking it. His employer knew of his addiction and gave him the choice of going to gamblers anonymous or prison.

After several years of therapy, he realised he had copied the pattern set down for him by his father.

He was honest with himself, and felt he could never be cured but was able to put a mechanism in place that allowed him to gamble with just 5% of his earnings, giving the rest to his wife for safekeeping.
****

Graphics designer, early fifties. Father was violent towards him, left home in his early teens as a result. Became an alcoholic and drug user. The self-destruct mode still causes him ill health and he's still unable to control his drinking habit.
****

TV repairman, early forties. Mother died when he was fourteen, was unaware she was dying and went into self-destruct mode out of guilt for not spending more time with her. Got into drugs, became uncaring about himself and others around him. Couldn't face who he'd become, borrowed money to feed his habit. Eventually faced his problem when money and friends ran out.

Gave up drugs and is now fully employed as a long distance lorry driver.
****

Gardener, late twenties. Adopted as a baby but never felt loved. Got into drugs, hard drugs and became an addict. Befriended vulnerable people, including recently bereaved in order to gain an advantage and

get access to their home to steal and feed his drug habit. Died of an overdose, aged 26.
****

Travel agent, mid thirties. Had a relationship with a man with mental problems. When she tried to sever the relationship he went to her home, waited for her to return, having first doused himself with petrol, which he then set alight. As a result, she was unable to work and as a single parent, with no earnings, she was targeted by a criminal element, becoming a drugs-dealer. Took drugs to forget. Still hooked but is now in full-time work and trying to leave her past behind.
****

Care worker early forties. Has abusive husband, builder by trade, between them they have three children. Needed 32 stitches in her neck after an argument where he hit her with a frying pan. Still with husband, who doesn't recognise he has a problem.
Daughter of above couple, left home at fifteen, had a series of abusive relationships. Got involved with a criminal element, fell pregnant to one of the members. Police became involved. Now lives in a safe house, after her life was threatened.
****

University graduate aged eighteen. Son of an abusive and controlling father, who during the day worked in the city for a large corporation but at home was a violent bully. On one occasion ran amok in the house with an axe. Son witnessed much of this behaviour. Eventually, the Father committed suicide. Son tried to come to terms with father's behaviour, but was frightened of repeating the pattern. Like his father he suffered from depression, which eventually led him to copy his father by committing suicide.
****

Engineer late fifties. Had an abusive, controlling father, who worked in the armed forces. His father sent him to military college at the age of ten, where he fell victim to abuse by other boys. Filled with shame he ran away and at the age of eighteen lived on the streets, where he met a man who befriended him and in return for favours took him to another country where he could find fame. All he had to do was pose for a few nude pictures. He carried out the man's wishes and accompanied him abroad. Eventually he married and had a daughter but beat his wife and abused his daughter to make them feel the pain he suffered.
He is still in denial and can't understand why his wife and daughter don't want anything to do with him.
****

Quantity surveyor, early fifties. Mother died when he was in his late teens. Had a controlling father, ex armed forces. Father remarried but marriage ended when he murdered his second wife. Son grew up to be controlling and abusive.
****

Builder, early thirties. Fancied his teenage cousin, kidnapped her, raped and murdered her. Afterwards committed suicide.
****

Forensic police medical officer, early fifties. Abused his authority, drugged and raped young girls who were left in his care.
****

Evolutionary consciousness is a process. As we battle our way through life's experiences another battle takes place inside, as we face our inner doubts, fears and demons.

Everyone has a story to tell, for each one of the above there are thousands more growing up in 'so called normal' environments, so don't be misled.
At the end of the day we are individuals first. The patterns we are taught by our parents are ones we use in our adult life, by recognising them we are able to make changes.

What is needed is a greater understanding through education, which will help build a safer environment for the children of tomorrow because without them there is no future.

Two of Britain's most literary lovers were Robert Browning and Elizabeth Barrett Browning.

Elizabeth was the daughter of a domineering father and it was rumoured she had suffered abuse. She was virtually bedridden until she met Robert, with whom she eloped to become part of Victorian England's greatest love story.

The Lady's Yes

'Yes,' I answered you last night;
'No,' this morning, sir I say :
Colours seen by candle-light
Will not look the same by day.

When the violas played their best,
Lamps above and laughs below,
Love me sounded like a jest,
Fit for yes or fit for no.

Call me false or call me free,
Vow, whatever light may shine, -
No man on your face shall see
Any grief for change on mine.

Yet the sin is on us both;
Time to dance is not to woo;
Wooing light makes fickle truth,
Scorn of me recoils on you.

Learn to win a lady's faith
Nobly, as the thing is high,
Bravely, as for life and death,
With a loyal gravity.

Lead her from the festive boards,
Point her to the starry skies;
Guard her, by your truthful words
Pure from courtship's flatteries.

By your truth she shall be true,
Ever true, as wives of yore;
And her yes, once said to you.
SHALL be Yes for evermore.

E.B. Browning

The aftermath

Women within abusive relationships often go on to have mental problems:

- Emotional abuse is like brainwashing
- Lack of self-confidence
- Lack of self-worth
- Nervous breakdowns
- Psychotic breakdown
- Shell shock or post traumatic stress syndrome
- Depression
- Drug abuse or dependency
- Weight loss or weight gain
- Attempts or thoughts of suicide
- Self harming
- Isolation takes them even further away from society
- The outside world becomes a scary place
- They are made to feel they deserve what happened and that they brought it upon themselves
- Trust becomes one of their biggest hurdles because they trusted enough to love someone who misused that love by abusing it.

75% of women that are killed by their abusive partners are murdered after they leave.

Children within abusive relationships often go on to have mental problems:

- Emotional abuse is like brainwashing
- Lack of self-confidence
- Lack of self-worth
- Nervous breakdowns
- Psychotic breakdown
- Shell shock or post traumatic stress syndrome
- Depression
- Drug abuse or dependency
- Weight loss or weight gain
- Attempts or thoughts of suicide
- Self harming
- Isolation takes them even further away from society
- The outside world becomes a scary place
- They are made to feel they deserve what happened and that they brought it upon themselves
- They think love is abuse.

Children learn from their parents
Children Learn What they live

If a child lives with criticism, he learns to condemn.
If a child lives with hostility, he learns to fight.
If a child lives with ridicule, he learns to be shy.
If a child lives with shame, he learns to feel guilty.
If a child lives with tolerance, he learns to be patient.
If a child lives with encouragement, he learns confidence.
If a child lives with praise, he learns to appreciate.
If a child lives with fairness, he learns justice.
If a child lives with security, he learns faith.
If a child lives with approval, he learns to like himself.
If a child lives with acceptance and friendship, he learns to find
love in the world.

Author unknown

The Lamb

Little lamb, who made thee?
Dost thou know who made thee?
Gave thee life, and bid thee feed,
By the stream and o'er the mead?
Gave thee clothing of delight,
Softest clothing, woolly, bright?
Gave thee such a tender voice,
Making all the vales rejoice?
Little Lamb, who made thee?
Dost thou know who made thee?

Little Lamb, I'll tell thee,
Little Lamb, I'll tell thee,
He is called by they name,
For he calls Himself a Lamb.
He is meek, and He is mild:
He became a little child.
I a child, and thou a lamb,
we are called by his name.
Little Lamb, God bless thee!
Little Lamb, God bless thee!
William Blake

Statistics show that a high percentage of single parents are women

Most of these families are living in poverty

Women in Britain were only allowed to take charge of their own income tax affairs in 1990

Men are still reluctant to give women long-term jobs because they expect women to leave to have children.

A MESSAGE
for
Basic Human Rights

It should be the goals of Education to strengthen communities by respecting people of varying backgrounds and beliefs.

Establishing a feeling of self-worth amongst those in the Community by offering a purpose in life through Ethnical and Spiritual values.

Respect should be given for Law and Order and the rights of others

Respect should be given for the individual to allow Justice, Fair play, Fundamental Rights, Responsibilities and above all Freedoms to flourish

**The easiest person to deceive is one's own self -
Edward Bulwer-Lytton**

Vengeance has no foresight - Napoleon Bonaparte

Delay of justice is injustice – Walter Savage Landor

FOOD FOR THOUGHT

Abuser inflicts pain onto victim by way of physical or mental torture

Children see the results

Children get upset because they see the pain on the victims face and ARE aware something is wrong

Repeat this pattern over and over again. As years go by the child/children accepts this as NORMAL behaviour

The child becomes aware of how the pain is inflicted and copy this in adulthood.

Imagine you own a dog

Each night when you come home from work, the dog runs up to greet you, wagging its tail.

You stroke the dog and enjoy the time you have together, which is mutually beneficial.

Imagine an abuser coming home, he sees the dog who runs up to greet him, wagging its tail, he screams and kicks the dog who retreats under the kitchen table and stays there for the rest of the evening.

In the morning he feels terrible and makes a fuss of the dog and the following evening comes home and takes the dog for a walk and enjoys his company, re-establishing the bond.
However, the following day he comes home, in a bad mood and lashes out at the dog, who scurries back to his refuge place under the kitchen table. This time the abuser doesn't notice, thus setting a pattern. From now on this becomes a regualr event whenever the abuser feels stressed or angry. If the dog reacts it gets a beating.

Eventually, the dog stays under the kitchen table

The dog becomes distrustful, even when the abuser is being nice, and thus lays the foundations of their relationship together because he failed to understand the dogs needs.

141

The dog will use its animal instincts to avoid punishment, and so sets the pattern for life together.

As a victim of the abuser's anger the dog becomes accepting of this behaviour, which gradually becomes the norm.

Look at the following and tick a or b, for your answer:

	a.	**b.**
What did the dog do wrong?	Nothing	Should not have greeted his master
Should he have ignored his master?	Yes	No
Should he have bitten his master when he was kicked?	Yes	No
What happens to the dog if he bites his master?	Beaten	Put down, Destroyed

Now carry out this test:

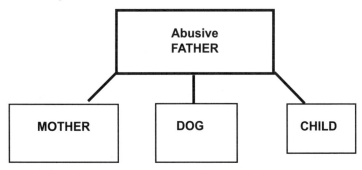

Examine the links above, then answer the following questions: For the purpose of this exercise, the father is shown as an abuser.

Which is the biggest box?	Father, Mother, Dog, Child
Which is the smallest box?	Father, Mother, Dog, Child
Where does the chain of command come from?	Father, Mother, Dog, Child
What do you think the father is demonstrating to the child by kicking the dog?	Power Authority Lack of control Just had a bad day Cruelty
Do you think it's the dog's fault	Yes No
If the father shouts at the mother and upsets her. Do you think that this is a good thing to do?	Yes No
If you remove the dog, do you think the father will pick on someone else?	Yes No
Who do you think that will be?	Mother, Child
Do you think the father feels better after getting rid of his anger?	Yes No Feels guilty Feels ashamed
Would you rather see the father understand his behaviour?	Yes No
Do you think the father enjoys getting angry?	Yes No

Whose fault is it afterwards?	Father Mother Child Dog
How would you class the father?	Cruel Kind Unhappy Happy Nice Strong Powerful Weak

Now look at the following:

1. Isolation	Cut off victims link to the outside world	Discourage victim from keeping in touch with friends or family
2.Exhaustion	Look for weaknesses and weaken the victims ability mentally and physically	Induced illness. Sleep deprivation, over exertion. This can lead to a psychotic breakdown and long term effects of such experiences are traumatic neuroses comparable to shell shock or post traumatic stress syndrome
3. Threats	Cause victim anxiety and despair by analysing and criticsing	Increase threats. Vague threats, threats against family or friends. Name calling
4. Be nice	Small treats and presents, maybe a weekend away	Victim becomes compliant and submissive again

5. Be aggressive	Keep up the work to weaken victims resolve	Victim talks of suicide and is suffering from depression
6. Be nice	But confuse victims thought processes. Decide how much abuse you want the victim to accept-psychological or physical	Victim has feelings of unreality and disorientation
7. Be controlling	Make victim believe they have done this to themselves but let them know, you are there to help. Substantiate this with a counsellor for example become the victim's guru	Victim tries to commit suicide
8. Ease up	Victim out of control. Accuse them of being mad. Don't forget to back this up by endorsing the fact that the counsellor, for example agrees with you	Victim fails in suicide attempt. Examine whether there has been outside intervention
9. Retreat	Let Victim recover. Give them a little treat	Start process again, should Victim attempt to get away
10. Last resort	Threaten Victim with violence and carry out threat, if this is successful, add it into the programme	Gradually increase violence, start with slapping If all goes wrong, kill victim, kill family, kill self

It may surprise you to know that some of these techniques are used to gain information under interrogation and many of them are used in an abusive relationship.

THE JOINT PERSPECTIVE –
What makes people angry

MARRIED MALE Aged between 20 – 30	MARRIED FEMALE Aged between 20 – 30
Often feel pressured into getting married and pressured into getting a good job, which offers stability	Also feel pressured into getting married, having children and keep working
When the children come along, the man feels trapped and torn between the pressures of work and his role within the family unit	Nowadays women try and fit work in around the family, so the added burden of balancing a happy home life with the pressures placed on them in the workplace
Traditionally, men expected their wives to stay at home and look after the house and children's needs	Women feel trapped in this existence. Often because they are unable to contribute financially and feel they are not respected for their mothering abilities.
When a man comes home from a long day at work, he isn't prepared for the development of the baby/child/children. Noise/ tantrums/ crying/illness and MESS. All of these add stress to any relationship	Many women feel isolated because they are left in charge of the children's welfare and are not free to leave the family home without making the necessary arrangements to have the children looked after. This can lead to resentment
Many men feel that they become a taxi driver and servant to the children's and often wife's needs	Women find socialising difficult due to restraints imposed by the children, this can sometimes lead to depression
Men traditionally take care of the heavy jobs around the home, gardening, DIY, maintenance.	Women traditionally do most of the housework, cooking, ironing, washing etc.

Men often have a more active social life outside the home, leaving the woman feeling further isolated	Women may become distrustful of their partners if they feel they are staying away from the home environment for longer than necessary
Men feel they don't have the ability to express themselves	Women naturally worry about their family as part of their nurturing and mothering instincts
Men feel the need to leave after arguments in order to give themselves space	Women just feel further trapped in the home
Men find it difficult to talk about their feelings, for fear of not being understood or because of their upbringing they feel it shows a weakness in their masculinity	Women feel the need to talk through problems and issues
Men often feel that women avoid sex and that his demands are not met	Women feel the need to have sex in a loving manner
Remember the saying : she's got a headache	Well, maybe she has. She's got a pretty full agenda
Financial restrictions. As men are often still the breadwinner, he worries about money issues and how much the family/ household bills are costing him to run.	Women earn less than men on average and sometimes feel awkward about asking for money
Remember the saying : Treat them mean to keep them keen.	Really? She'll just wait till the children are old enough and leave
Constant arguments can lead to a strain on the relationship and a breakdown in communication follows	Try and mend problems/ issues, talk them through, don't let things fester

If communication has broken down completely, this makes way for other emotions that could be destructive to the relationship	By avoiding subjects because they are too painful you lead to the decline of the relationship. One of women's biggest complaints is that he doesn't want to talk about it.
Men always have a friend who can advise them what to do:-	Women also have friends who can advise them what to do:-
- Sounds like she's got a bit of a problem if you ask me	- Leave him with the children, then he'll know what its like
- Join the gym	- Join the gym
- Forget her, women are not worth it	- Forget him, he'll never understand
- She just needs a good slap, she just needs a good slap, she just needs	- I bet he's already found someone else.
- Debbie's available why don't you just get on with your own life	- He's not worth it.
- Throw her out - Leave her	- Men only think of one thing - Leave him, leave him, leave......
- She needs a slap	-Leave him

Lack of communication, respect, apathy, busy lives, **familiarity breeds contempt**. Whatever the excuse, the meaning of family is lacking in today's society. As far as children are concerned, they need a real sense of belonging if they are to go on and have families of their own, so it is important to teach them values which they can rely on in adulthood. Those childhood memories are the ones they will reflect on when they become parents, so it is vital they have stability to equip them for the emotional rollercoaster of life

Strip away greed, avarice, selfishness, anger, **'the grass is often greener on the other side of the fence'** syndrome (which is often not the case), and you will find more understanding and compassion which can lead to a better lifestyle for all concerned.

The future is not in your hands because you can not change things, but the present is a gift, that is why it is called present.

THE SOLUTION

This can be a long process as you become conditioned to accepting abuse and may not recognise it a second time round. Here is one way of putting matters right for both parties:

MALE	FEMALE
Try to communicate in a constructive manner	Communication is the key to any relationship but you probably don't want to say too much at first
Accept change and learn to compromise. Talk with her in a way that doesn't leave her feeling threatened	Offer a solution Women want to talk without being scared of verbal or physical attack
Don't be judgmental – listen to what she says	Voice your opinions, when you feel safe to do so
Accept ownership of your problems and acknowledge them	Get him to tell you about himself Fill in the check box and speak with friends
Know what resources are available in the area so you can help	When you feel comfortable you can talk about your experiences. Test the ground and see what his reaction is
Believe her experiences, try and understand how she must have felt	If he comes back at you, saying that his friends think you are badly damaged and that no one else would have you, start thinking of terminating the relationship.
Respect her confidentiality	If, after telling him an experience, he begins to laugh or if you find his friends start treating you differently, you are on the road to an abusive relationship.

Encourage her, there are many women who have suffered in this way.	See how considerate he is to your feelings
Never ask too many questions, let her tell you when she's ready and set some time aside for this	Watch out for the 'self destruct' button, this can be overwhelming when you start to realise what happened to you and that you didn't deserve it.
Never think she deserved it, no one deserves to be abused	Reassure yourself, feel comfortable with your emotions
Keep her positive, shame and guilt of what has happened to her are heavy burdens to carry for anyone, let alone an innocent victim	Plan things with your partner which include friends and family
Respect any decisions she wishes to make in her own life	You can begin to feel comfortable in expressing yourself
Value her opinions	Your experience has made you what you are
She is special. Love unconditionally	That makes you special Love unconditionally without fear
ONGOING	
Talk through money issues that are mutually beneficial	You are not less of a person just because you earn less
Share parenting. Being a positive non-violent person is an ideal environment for children to flourish	Allow shared parenting, let children become part of the family unit
Be open, honest. Speak truthfully	Be open, honest. Speak truthfully
Accept responsibility for yourself	Accept responsibility for yourself Acknowledge past violence

Acknowledge past violence Make decisions for the family jointly Encourage the children with their emotional development. Remember this is a family Help them understand, so they don't repeat the patterns You can all learn from this process	Encourage children to participate in family activities. Do not allow them to feel isolated Every time they experience abuse, they become confused. Help them understand, so they don't repeat the patterns You can all learn from this process

The definition of love is:

Warm affection and devotion,
attachment,
liking, or fondness,
paternal benevolence

Those who love deeply cannot age – Arthur Wing Pinero

The important message is:
We need to build a Safe, Just and Tolerant Society

FACT

Domestic Violence is chronically under reported,

- Claims 150 lives each year

- Accounts for a quarter of all violent crimes

- An average of 35 assaults occur before a victim calls the Police

- Claims the lives of two women each week

- Costs in excess of £5 Billion a year

Check for the most up todate figures:
www.homeoffice.gov.uk/crime/domesticviolence/

And where children are present, what future harm do you imagine it does to them?

- One woman in four experiences domestic violence at some stage in her life (The Women's unit, 1999)

- 93% of incidents of domestic violence are carried out by men against women. (SERICC)

- Most rapes happen indoors, in homes – only 9% take place outside in dark alleys, late at night (SERICC)

- 83% of women who are raped are raped by men they know including 20% by boyfriends and 33% by husbands (SERICC)

- An incident of domestic violence happens every 20 seconds in the UK – all over the country in every type of family (Stanko, 2000)

- Domestic violence accounts for almost a quarter (23%) of all violent crime. The British Crime Survey: England and Wales (London: Home office, 2000)

GOOD NEWS

'The Domestic Violence, Crime and Disorder Act, 2004', described as the biggest overhaul of Domestic Violence legislation in 30 years.
The Bill received its long awaited Royal Assent on 15th November 2004 and is heralded as signalling a new era for both the victims of crime and witnesses of crime.
The Act aims to strengthen the rights of victims and witnesses.

More importantly, the Act contains many new measures which should make it much more straightforward and help give both victims and witnesses to crimes the confidence which is needed to come forward to report crimes of domestic violence'. (Rights of Women)

25 Specialist Domestic Violence Courts have been set up across England and Wales.

Domestic Violence is a Crime

SELF CONFIDENCE CHART - Use this as a progress chart, which will tell you where you are at the moment and gradually you can build on this to regain your self-confidence (**You may wish to photocopy these pages before you begin**)

PROGRESS SCALE NAME	DATE STARTED .... DAY						
	1	2	3	4	5	6	7
1. I feel tense and wound up:							
Most of the time							
A lot of the time							
Time to time, occasionally							
Not at all							
2. I still enjoy the things I used to enjoy:							
Definitely as much							
Not quite as much							
Only a little							
Hardly at all							
3. I get sort of frightened as if something awful is going to happen:							
Very definitely and very badly							
Yes, but not too badly							
A little, but it doesn't worry me							
Not at all							
4. I can laugh and see the funny side of things:							
As much as I always could							
Not quite as much now							
Definitely not as much now							
Not at all							
5. Worrying thoughts go through my mind:							
A great deal of the time							
A lot of the time							
From time to time but not too often							
Only occasionally.							

Progress Scale Page 2	1	2	3	4	5	6	7
6. I feel cheerful:							
Not at all							
Not often							
Sometimes							
Most of the time							
7. I can sit at ease and feel relaxed:							
Definitely							
Usually							
Not often							
Not at all							
8. I feel as if I am slowed down:							
Nearly all the time							
Very often							
Sometimes							
Most of the time							
9. I get a sort of frightened feeling like butterflies in my stomach:							
Not at all							
Occasionally							
Quite often							
10. I have lost interest in my appearance:							
Definitely							
I don't take as much care as I should							
I may not take as much care							
I take just as much care as ever.							
11. I feel restless as if I have been on the move							
Very much indeed							
Quite a lot							
Not very much							
Not at all							
12. I look forward with enjoyment to things:							
As much as I ever did							
Rather less than I used to							
Definitely less than I used to							
Hardly at all							
13. I get sudden feelings of panic:							
Very often indeed							

Progress Scale	Page 3	1	2	3	4	5	6	7
Quite often								
Not very often								
Not at all								
14. I can enjoy a good book, radio, TV programme								
Often								
Sometimes								
Not often								
Very seldom								
15. I don't go out:								
Sometimes								
Not often								
Very seldom								
Not at all								
Quite a lot								

Building your self-confidence may take some time, by filling in this chart you will gradually identify areas you need to work on. So believe in yourself, take charge of your life and learn from your experiences, that have made you the special person you are today.

Those who cannot remember the past are condemned to repeat it
George Santayana, The life of Reason, Volume 1, 1905.